E VIEW

DING

- California.

?0, on S. P. R. R. to OREGON.

NTS OF

t Board of Trade

California.

Key to Prominent Places.

33. McCormick, Saeltzer Co.
34. Presbyterian Church.
35. M. E. Church.
36. Redding Gas Work.
37. Catholic Church.
38. Catholic Cemetery.
39. R. R. Hotel.
30. R. R. Depot.
31. Redding Planing Mill.
32. Democrat Office.
33. County Court House.
34. Hotel Del Monte.
35. Reservoir.
36. Public School.
37. Protestant Cemetery.
38. Free Bridge.
39. Res. of H. F. Johnson.
40. " Judge C. C. Bush.
41. " J. M. Gleaves.
42. " Hon A. Bell.
43. " H. R. Wiley.
44. " R. Bostwick.

Shasta County at the present time, is the most progressive county north of San Francisco.

It is the center of population, trade and travel of Northern California.

It is the Geographical center of that large portion of the State north of Marysville.

There are 300 clear days and 65 rainy ones each year.

The Towns of the County are all flourishing.

Redding, the County Seat has a Population 3500. This city contains the largest business houses in the State north of San Francisco. It has excellent school buildings, churches, &c. Buildings to cost $900,000 are projected for the season of 1889. It is the proposed intersecting point for the Union Pacific and California and Oregon Railroads.

Anderson a beautiful town of 1500 people is surrounded by immense areas of young orchard and vineyard.

Cottonwood, a thriving town of 700 inhabitants, is in a fertile farming section.

Millville is a town of 500 people, located in the center of a rich agricultural district.

Falls City, 400 inhabitants, is in the beautiful Fall River Valley, the future Lowell of the Pacific Coast.

Sewazey is one of the new towns in a rich farming country.

Igo and Ono are two small towns 5 miles apart, near the S. W. boundary of the County.

For Scenery, there is Sacramento and Pit river canons, the falls of the Fall River, Mt Shasta and Lassen Peaks, 90 miles distant, Burney and Clover Creek Falls, beautiful Lakes, Hot and Sulphur Springs, &c.

Some may equal but none excel Shasta, in the natural resources to make a prosperous county and a successful, contented and happy people.   [OVER]

REDDING
&SHASTA
COUNTY
Gateway to the Cascades

REDDING & SHASTA COUNTY
Gateway to the Cascades

An Illustrated History by John D. Lawson

Picture research by Tom Dunlap
Partners in Progress by Richard Kelly

Produced in cooperation with the
Greater Redding Chamber of Commerce

Windsor Publications, Inc.
Northridge, California

To my dear wife,
Clara,
who helped with the rough edges
and
put up with my moods,
and to all those pioneering spirits, past and present
who settled
Shasta County, created Redding,
and helped both to grow and prosper
this book is fondly dedicated.

Windsor Publications, Inc.—History Book Division

Publisher: John M. Phillips
Editorial Director: Teri Davis Greenberg
Design Director: Alexander E. D'Anca

Staff for *Redding & Shasta County: Gateway to the Cascades*
Senior Editor: Gail Koffman
Editorial Development: Karl Stull
Assistant Editors: Laura Cordova, Marilyn Horn
Director, Corporate Biographies: Karen Story
Assistant Director, Corporate Biographies: Phyllis Gray
Editor, Corporate Biographies: Judith L. Hunter
Layout Artist, Corporate Biographies: Mari Catherine Preimesberger
Sales Representatives, Corporate Biographies: Carter Reynolds, Margaret Reynolds
Editorial Assistants: Kathy M. Brown, Marcie Goldstein, Pam Juneman, Pat Pittman
Proofreader: Susan J. Muhler
Designer: J.R. Vasquez
Layout Artist, Editorial: Michele Ficks-Hellman

Library of Congress Cataloging-in-Publication Data

Lawson, John 1927-
    Redding & Shasta County: gateway to the Cascades.

    Bibliography: p. 180
    Includes index.
    1. Shasta County (Calif.)—History. 2. Redding
(Calif.)—History. 3. Shasta County (Calif.)—
Description and travel. 4. Shasta County (Calif.)—
Industries. 5. Redding (Calif.)—Description.
6. Redding (Calif.)—Industries. I. Title.
F868.S49L39 1986   979.4'24   86-22375
ISBN 0-89781-187-9

Endpapers: *This artist's conception of an aerial view of Redding was drawn in 1888. It is geographically accurate as to the placement of buildings, streets, and the Sacramento River. In this northeasterly view, the railroad tracks can be seen traversing from upper left to lower right. Courtesy, Redding Museum*

Opposite page: *Automobiles were not only a source of transportation in the 1920s but also a form of recreation. Clubs were formed for outings and socializing on wheels became a trend of the day. This group of automobile enthusiasts lined up for a photograph in front of the Empire Hotel in French Gulch. Courtesy, Shasta State Historic Park and Courthouse Museum*

CONTENTS

Foreword 8

Introduction 9

CHAPTER I:
Indian Country, Gold Country 11

CHAPTER II:
The Rush for Riches 25

CHAPTER III:
Progress at Poverty Flat 41

CHAPTER IV:
A Time of Promise 55

CHAPTER V:
Water Empowers the County 67

CHAPTER VI:
Forests Bring Big Business 81

CHAPTER VII:
Recreation Brings People 95

CHAPTER VIII:
Centennial in the Sun 115

CHAPTER IX:
Partners in Progress 135

Bibliography 180   Index 181

Acknowledgments

I am indebted to many sources, individuals, and institutions for help with this book.

Thanks is due primarily to the Shasta County Library, which granted use of its Boggs research section on local history, and to the *Record Searchlight*, which allowed use of its computer for organizing the text and its extensive clip file for research.

The Shasta Historical Park and the Redding Museum Art Center also provided much help in obtaining information and old prints, as did the Shasta Historical Society with its past issues of the *Covered Wagon*.

Sources of great help are mentioned in the bibliography. Primary ones consulted were the works of Edward Petersen, Mae Helene Bacon Boggs, Rosena Giles, Myrtle McNamar, and Charles Gleeson. The California State Library in Sacramento was also a valuable resource.

Among individuals, I owe much to the patience and understanding of my wife, Clara, who gave up many hours of companionship to the engrossing task of research and writing.

I am indebted beyond measure to retired Judge Richard B. Eaton, who proofread the manuscript, corrected it where necessary, and offered much helpful information and advice, drawing on his knowledge and experience of many years. Thanks are also due to Milton Black for his reading of the manuscript.

Others due recognition for support and encouragement when needed include co-workers Tom Dunlap and Richard Kelly; the *Record-Searchlight*'s editor Robert W. Edkin and business manager Larry Wakefield; Don Shirley, who undertook chairmanship of Friends of Shasta County Libraries while I worked on this project; Windsor Publications editors Gail Koffman and Karl Stull; County Librarian Diane Duquette; Ann Hunt, who chaired the Shasta County Historical Society; Writers Forum (formerly the Redding Writers Club) members; and many other colleagues and friends, especially Lou Gerard, Jr., Rufus Knapp, Hank Woodrum, Dan Cherry, Charlotte Engle, Vic Woodard, Angie Seigle, Lawre Myers, Gerald Akin, and Veryl Oakland. Space does not permit a total listing of all who should be mentioned.

As with all enterprises of this nature there are bound to be errors and omission, for which I beg the reader's indulgence.

Lassen Peak and Chaos Crags are silhouetted on the horizon as the sun rises over the Sacramento River. Photo by Robert McKenzie

Foreword

Shasta County, established in 1850, was one of the original twenty-seven counties of California. Before this time, the area had known the footprints of its native peoples, of Jedediah Smith and of Hudson's Bay Company trappers, of its first settler, Major Pierson Barton Reading, and of the argonauts who came in the Gold Rush year of 1849. The gold mining era, centered in the town of Shasta, flourished in the 1850s and dwindled in the 1860s while Redding was yet unborn.

Then in 1872, the Central Pacific Railroad, constructing a line toward Portland, built a temporary railhead at the head of the Sacramento Valley and called it Redding—named not for Major Reading but for B.B. Redding of Sacramento, general land agent of the railroad. Redding remained this railhead until 1883, when the line was extended up the Sacramento River Canyon; but even after this, Redding continued to be a major shipping point. The new town's growth led to its incorporation in 1887, and to its succeeding Shasta as county seat in 1888.

In this book author John Lawson has commemorated the city of Redding and its surroundings. The text is a rich tapestry of historical data for those who know the county and the city as they are now, and are curious about how they came to be. Most now living in the area have come here in recent years and can both enjoy and benefit from a look at its development during its first one hundred years.

Richard B. Eaton
Historian
Redding, California

Introduction

Every May a curious procession streams past thousands of spectators in downtown Redding to celebrate Rodeo Week.

And every December hundreds of caroling children roll by on flatbed trucks festooned with evergreens to open the Christmas shopping season.

From fancy-dressed cowboys astride well-groomed horses to angelic sprites marching with tightly held candles may seem like a quantum leap in logic. It's not for Redding, which is and always has been a city of contradictions and contrasts.

A city of some 51,000 people by recent count, Redding lies astride the Sacramento River about 160 miles north of the state capitol in Sacramento and 230 miles north of San Francisco. It is the county seat of Shasta County, a 3,858-square-mile area bordered by Siskiyou, Modoc, Lassen, Plumas, Tehama, and Trinity counties.

The city of Redding is a trade hub for Northern California and Southern Oregon, drawing from a multi-county area of some 250,000 people, according to a recent federal estimate. Redding also serves as a gateway to the Cascade and Trinity Alps recreation areas, and as the hub of north-south Interstate 5 and two east-west state highways, 299 and 44.

Redding is also the seat of government for Shasta County, a wildly beautiful landscape of mountain, meadow, woodland, and plain that complements the city with its irresistible appeal to a wide variety of physical, social, cultural, and artistic interests.

Like the hub of a giant wheel, Shasta sends its spokes of influence from Redding northward to Lakehead and Castella; northeast to McArthur, Burney, and Fall River Mills, then closer to Round Mountain and Montgomery Creek, and southeast to Manton.

The remainder of the wheel finds Cottonwood to the south, then the spokes go southeast to Igo, Ono, and Platina, including the growing community of Olinda in Happy Valley; and west to Whiskeytown, northwest to French Gulch, Shasta, and Keswick.

An inner rim sends Redding's spokes of county government to the northern suburban communities of Mountain Gate, Summit City, and Central Valley; eastward to Bella Vista and Palo Cedro and beyond to Oak Run, Whitmore, Millville, and Shingletown; then south to Anderson, the county's only other incorporated city.

Like Redding, the county, too, has its contrasts. One might find cowboys herding cattle near Whitmore, beekeepers in Bella Vista, miners still looking for nuggets around French Gulch, and loggers in Shingletown.

If poet Carl Sandburg once called Chicago a "city of big shoulders," Redding might be called a "city of big forearms"—for pulling lumber, running jackhammers, roping cattle, and holding mining drills. But Redding is also a city of flexible fingers, operating keyboards of typewriters and computers, as well as tuning musical instruments and operating high-tech equipment.

Therein lies a paradox. While Redding in recent years has strived to become an urban center cultivating high-tech and other light industry, it still depends primarily on three major industries: wood products, agriculture, and recreation.

During the Rodeo Week parade the city both recalls its wild and woolly past as it celebrates a more even-tempered present. Yet in December, it is quite another story—the gingerbread land of retail fantasy competes with a religious outpouring of Redding's many churches in a parade that also represents the changing community. This parade captures the new Redding: ready to shuck its rudimentary frontier garments and settle down to genteel living and leisure pursuits.

Opposite page: Redding has always loved a parade. This circa 1915 parade shown here was moving west along Yuba Street between Market and California streets. Courtesy, Maida Glover Gandy

Indian Country, Gold Country

Redding sits like an island of urbanity in a wilderness of raw mountain peaks and rugged foothills, a panoramic tableaux that includes two of the state's highest peaks.

Directly to the east one can almost see where the volcanic Cascade mountain range merges into the northern Sierra. To the north are the three Shastas— towering Mt. Shasta, 14,162 feet high, Shasta Lake with its 365 miles of shoreline, and massive Shasta Dam, its spillway higher than Niagara Falls. To the east is rugged Lassen Peak, 10,457 feet high, one of the few active volcanoes in the United States. Both Shasta and Lassen form the southern linchpins of the sprawling Cascade range, part of the volcanic "Ring of Fire" that includes Crater Lake and Mt. Hood in Oregon and Washington's Mt. St. Helens.

Redding itself dominates a wide river valley of rolling grassland, three times the size of Rhode Island, accented by forested foothills, sidestreams and lakes.

At one time much of the north state was under water. Fossils of bygone marine life actually have been found inside the city limits. Geologic theories hold that mountain-building epochs of the past created the north state by pushing up land masses from the ocean floor. Certainly this might account for the minerals that have kept mining a backbone industry in the region since the Gold Rush.

The original residents of the region were, of course, the Indians, living in a network of tribal cultures dominated by the Wintu, who occupied the west bank of the Sacramento River on land that now includes Redding. The Wintu lived peacefully and quietly as they faced the seasons that roared down from the north,

The golden hues of autumn highlight a Quaking Aspen with Mt. Lassen in the background. Photo by Robert W. Small

These six Wintu males are wearing a cultural blend of clothing as they pose in the late 1800s for Redding photographer Louis Altpeter. This photograph was taken on Diestelhorst Flat near Reid's Ferry, where several Native Americans had gathered for a tribal dance event. Courtesy, Shasta Historical Society

their brown bodies shivering in their huts and long-houses during the cold, wet, windy winters, and burning during the long summer days when the sun was a molten ball of lava in a cloudless sky.

The Wintu found game aplenty—deer that ran in droves in the uplands and salmon that swam so thick in summer that one could cross the river in dry moccasins by stepping on their backs. The Wintu kept watch on the salmon runs and drove off braves of other tribes who tried to poach in their domain.

In the summers the Wintu ate edible plants and killed small game. They speared salmon and used bows and arrows to bring down deer, drying the carcasses to strips of jerky to sustain them through the long winter days when fruits and berries were scarce.

They bartered for goods with their neighbors, the Shastas and Modocs to the northwest, the Yana to the east, and the Atsugewi (Hat Creek) and Achomawi (Pit River) to the northeast. The Pit River, in fact, was so named because the Achomawi Indians devised ingenious animal traps by digging gourd-like pits and lining their bottoms with upturned, sharpened sticks.

Above: *Num-Ken-Chata, photographed here in 1931, was a Wintu woman in her native Shasta County hills in the vicinity of what is now Shasta Lake. She is wearing part of the same costume she wore years earlier as a young debutante: a hawk feather and snake rattler necklace, shell beads, buzzard feather fan, and a bead and yellow-hammer feather headdress. Courtesy, Lake Shasta Caverns*

Above, left: *This Pit woman and her two children are shown circa 1900 wearing an assortment of tribal as well as store-bought clothing. Members of the Pit River tribe lived along the riverbank from its origin at the northeast corner of the state, near Alturas, to the point where it enters the Sacramento River north of Redding in what is now Shasta Lake. Courtesy, Shasta Historical Society*

Unlike the Achomawi, who were frequently raided by the warlike Modocs to the north, the Wintu seemed to enjoy a relatively strife-free existence, bartering goods and trinkets and enjoying safety in numbers. But sometimes tribal rules and rituals broke down and relations turned into open warfare.

The Wintu's only adversaries of note were the Yana, who feared them and who occupied a narrow strip of land on the east side of the river.

The two tribes fought to dominate Bloody Island, a reedy island in the river near where Major Pierson Barton Reading later built his adobe. For the most part, however, the Indians respected tribal boundaries and mingled during seasonal celebrations, which were times for socializing and politicking among chieftains and their councils.

Curiously, the Indians seemed to avoid the mud-caked deltas and red clay cliffs at the bend in the river that came to be known as Poverty Flat. They may have had good reason to do so. Tales spread of a mysterious fever, possibly malaria, which afflicted those who tried to live near the stagnant water pools. There

Above: *The 1855 battle of Castle Crags, fought in these rocks, was the last battle between Indians and whites in the county in which the Indians used bows and arrows. Photo by Robert McKenzie*

Right: *Trojan Horse Rock is the name of this interesting Castle Crags rock formation. Photo by Robert McKenzie*

Above: *Robert McKenzie took this photograph of the Sacramento River's Red Banks.*

Left: *The historic Diestelhorst Bridge, built in 1915, is reflected in the waters of the Sacramento River. Photo by Robert McKenzie*

Renowned poet Cincinnatus "Joaquin" Miller worked in the mining camps of Shasta County for most of his youth. When he was fourteen years old he was wounded in the 1855 Battle of Castle Crags. Courtesy, Cirker's Dictionary of American Portraits

was also something called the "bloody flux" which could strike down a strong young brave like no rival warrior could. So they avoided the area although it offered access to the gravel shoals where the dying salmon spawned their young.

Another, more compelling reason, may have been the terrible floods which swept away hut and longhouse alike after torrential rains sent surges of muddy water down the Pit, McCloud, and Sacramento rivers. Woe be it to the Indian who, in reckless confidence under the summer sun, built his dwelling near the bank of the fickle Sacramento, especially at Poverty Flat.

The white settlers from the East brought with them a counterculture that clashed immediately with the Indians' way of life. When the immigrants arrived on horseback or muleback, with their rough, wooden, canvas-topped wagons and their livestock, the Indians sensed a danger to everything they valued beneath the sun, moon, and stars.

The first incursions, however, were peaceful. Indians for the most part were intrigued by the intruders and cooperated with them.

The first to arrive were explorers like Jedediah Smith, John Work, and Alexander McLeod, who pushed over the uncharted territory with small groups of men. Smith's party crossed the Sacramento River near Red Bluff, then headed northwest across the far corner of what is now Shasta County and into future Trinity County in 1828.

The Mad River was supposedly named by Smith after a heated argument he got into with Indians over the cost of crossing the southern Trinity County stream by canoe.

Exploration generally took several routes: south from Fort Vancouver at the mouth of the Columbia River in the Northwest Territory; west on the Oregon Trail through Nevada and Idaho into Northern California; and north from Yerba Buena and Sutter's Fort (now San Francisco and Sacramento).

Mt. Shasta is believed to have been named by Russian explorers from Fort Ross on the Pacific coast, who called it after their word for "chaste" or "white." Others have said Peter Ogden, an explorer who journeyed into the region in 1827, named the area after the Sastika or Shasta Indians, blood brothers and sisters of the Modocs, in southern Siskiyou County. Joaquin Miller, the poet of the Sierra who in his youth spent considerable time prospecting in Shasta County, once described the mountain as "lonely as God and white as a winter moon." Miller was wounded in sight of the mountain in the Battle of Castle Crags of 1855, reportedly the last battle between Indians and whites in which bows and arrows were used. He was then fourteen years of age.

Alexander McLeod, a trapper with the Hudson's Bay Company, brought a party through southern Siskiyou County in 1829, finding plenty of game for pelts. McLeod's name went astray—as Major Reading's name would suffer the same fate later—the town later established became McCloud.

As the trails became known, the explorers were followed by others: sheepherders who brought their flocks to the upper Sacramento Valley; adventurous settlers, lured by a promise of a land of sunshine and plenty; and naturalists seeking new ground for exploration.

The Wintu responded readily to the newcomers at first. Major Reading praised their work at Rancho Buena Ventura, where he put them on the payroll but treated them much like plantation slaves.

But as the migrants' numbers increased, the more they threatened the complex ecology of the Indians' lands and the greater the tensions grew.

Trappers took the young animals that meant so much to Indian livelihood. Sheep grazed the green shoots of spring, nibbling the grasslands that attracted deer. Deer were shot for sport as much as fodder, and the intruders clubbed salmon in the shallows.

Captain John C. Frémont, then a brash young topographical engineer with the army, brought an expedition from Sutter's Fort through the north state in 1846, engaging Indians in several skirmishes with some loss of life on both sides. It is believed that Frémont camped by Cottonwood Creek on the county's present southern boundary, and that his troops, like the warring Wintu and Yana tribes, also fought a "Battle of Bloody Island."

Redding historian James Dotta, who researched the island's history, doubts that the battle actually occurred. Writing in the *Covered Wagon,* the official publication of the Shasta Historical Society, Dotta said the account may have been embellished by overzealous campaigners in Frémont's 1856 bid for the Republican presidential nomination. Whether the battle was fought or not, hostilities between the Indians and whites grew, especially after the discovery of gold.

Word of gold's discovery spread like a virus after

Captain John C. Frémont brought an expedition from Sutter's Fort through the north state in 1846. He supposedly camped by Cottonwood Creek, near the county's present southern border. Courtesy, Cirker's Dictionary of American Portraits

Swiss John A. Sutter was behind Major Reading's exploration of Shasta County. He had requested Reading to lead a trapping expedition to map a route into the north state. Courtesy, Cirker's Dictionary of American Portraits

Although Philip Henry Sheridan became a Union Army general in the Civil War, his early service in the military led him to California where he was a lieutenant. It was at Fort Reading where Sheridan initiated his dominance; a few years later he was promoted to captain, and then to general, for his prudent leadership. Courtesy, Cirker's Dictionary of American Portraits

Like Philip Sheridan, John Bell Hood's career began at Fort Reading. He went on to become a famous Civil War general in the Confederate Army. Courtesy, Cirker's Dictionary of American Portraits

Marshall's find at Sutter's Mill in Coloma. The Gold Rush brought hundreds of miners to Shasta County after Major Reading, a friend and confidant of Sutter, learned of the discovery at Coloma and ordered his Indian ranch workers to pan for the elusive metal in streams that trickled across his sprawling land grant.

Gold was discovered at Reading's Bar on Clear Creek, and the word got out despite the Major's frantic efforts to keep it a secret. Would-be miners swarmed into the north state by the hundreds, sleeping by night in bedrolls under the stars, living in tents or rude shanties of scrap lumber, and working their claims by day. They washed gravel in the gurgling streams with pans and sluiceboxes in the early spring, then burrowed into the dry, hard-clay hillsides after summer dried the streambeds.

The Indians viewed the constant roiling of streams with growing resentment, knowing the murkiness threatened the salmon runs. They also resented the miners' constant foraging of deer and other edibles that were their staples of existence. The clash of cultures led to intermittent violence.

The Castle Crags battle of 1855 culminated three years of clashes between Indians and intruding settlers and goldseekers. Various accounts indicate that Shasta Indians ambushed a group of whites—either a party of gold miners or a wagon train. Vengeful whites formed a posse and drove the Indians into the recesses of the granite crags, which tower 6,500 feet high and now form the scenic attraction of a state park.

The Shastas rained arrows on their tormentors, then fled after stashing $40,000 in captured gold from the raid somewhere in the rugged peaks. Legend has it that the gold remains hidden to this day.

Elsewhere, the clashes of Indians and the newcomers were localized and sporadic.

In a series of encounters that became known as the "Salmon Wars," one of the more tragic episodes occurred in 1864 when a band of Indians slaughtered most of the William Allen family. Only a four-year-old boy and Allen himself were spared. Allen, a rancher, found the bodies of his loved ones when he returned home from work.

A posse of forty ranchers from the Millville, Oak Run, and Balls Ferry areas killed eighty to 100 Indians in the skirmish that followed. Angry ranchers waded the river and, splitting into two groups, surrounded an Indian encampment on the large oval island near the

Captain Jack was the leader of a band of Modoc Indians who were involved in many skirmishes with white settlers and the U.S. Army. The final battles were fought in what is now the Lava Beds National Monument during the years 1872 to 1873. He was hanged by the Army in 1873. Courtesy, Shasta State Historic Park Courthouse Museum

mouth of what is now Battle Creek. Someone friendly to the Indians fired a shot to warn them, but it was too late.

Another tragedy resulted when Marie Dersch, wife of George Dersch, was shot and mortally wounded by Indians during a raid August 20, 1866, as she was running through an orchard to protect her children. The Dersch children, Fred and Annie, were walking with their blind uncle, Frederick Dersch, who came to Shasta County in 1855 from Bavaria and prospected on Clear Creek until he lost his sight in 1861. After Mrs. Dersch died, vengeful white settlers pursued the Indians, killing many.

Little was done to forestall worsening relations. Dr. O.M. Wozencroft in 1851 managed to put together a treaty with subtribes, with the help of Major Reading (whom the Indians called "Shaktu," or "Great Chief") and a Major McWhinney of the U.S. Bureau of Indian Affairs. But it was among eighteen in California that were never ratified.

Renegade whites added to the turmoil by assuming Indian guise to attack miners on their claims near Yreka. Miners held a mass meeting at Shasta in April 1852 to swear vengeance but with 5,300 Indians outnumbering whites almost four to one, it was unsafe to stray far from communities.

Settlers appealed to Fort Reading for help, but, with less than 100 men, the fort was little more than a place to raise the flag in the vast north state wilderness. Established in May 1852 on Cow Creek a few miles from the Sacramento River near Major Reading's rancho, the fort nourished the careers of two men who later became famous Civil War generals—Lieutenants Philip H. Sheridan of the Union Army and John B. Hood, who fought for the Confederacy.

During the Civil War, most residents of the Shasta area supported the North, possibly because of the blue-coated presence at Fort Reading. A relatively large contingent enlisted in the Union Army but saw only limited frontier duty in Arizona. Only a few county residents actually made it to the war zone in the South and East.

The fort played host to an assembly of Indians desiring peace in 1854 because of widespread starvation among the tribes. Soldiers and settlers alike responded to the emergency with food and supplies, but relations later worsened again. A pitched battle was fought between 150 Indians and thirty settlers at Buncombe's

Mill, later called Millville. Other skirmishes took place near Cottonwood and French Gulch.

Despite such unrest and tragedies like the Allen massacre, the federal government practically abandoned Fort Reading in 1857 and deactivated it in 1866, possibly because of cutbacks to offset the excesses of spending during the Civil War.

Horrifying as the Allen and Dersch conflicts were, they paled before the prolonged struggle known as the Modoc Wars.

The town of Redding was caught up in one of the last campaigns of the U.S. Army against Indians. The new town became a staging ground for supplies sent to the troops of General Edward R.S. Canby. (According to some sources, Canby was the only general ever killed by Indians during hostilities. Civil War Brevet Brigadier General George Armstrong Custer had the rank of lieutenant colonel when he was killed in the Battle of the Little Big Horn.)

Kientepoos, or "Captain Jack," a rebel Modoc chieftain, led a band of Modocs against Canby's federal troops for several years after the government failed to sign the treaty of 1864 negotiated by old Schonchin, chief of the Modocs and Kientepoos' father.

Under Captain Jack, Modoc warriors began to raid wagon trains and ranches in the 1850s. In 1852 they attacked an immigrant train of sixty-five people near Tule Lake, killing all but two teenaged girls, who were spared, and a man who escaped. The tragedy became known thereafter as the "Massacre of Bloody Point."

Whites retaliated two months later with the Ben Wright massacre of November 1852, wiping out a village of forty-six Modocs. The five escapees included Schonchin John, brother of the old chief, who never forgot the slaughter. He became second in command to Captain Jack, who was also advised by a wily shaman (medicine man) called Curly-Headed Doctor.

Full-scale warfare followed, including the Castle Crags battle (the Modocs were a splinter group of the sympathetic Shastas then). Muddled federal administration of Indian problems and outright corruption among some Indian agents kept the hostilities alive through the 1860s with skirmishes and disputes over treaties.

Judge Elisha Steele of Yreka negotiated the treaty of 1864, which did not bind the Modocs to reservation life, but it wasn't ratified. A second treaty, which was ratified, required them to give up their tribal lands and live on a reservation.

Ensuing warfare included sporadic skirmishes and frustrating searches by cavalry troops in attempts to force the Modocs to surrender. After each encounter the Indians seemed to vanish into the desolate landscape, hiding in lava caves.

Finally General Canby and several representatives of the settlers called a truce, inviting Captain Jack, Schonchin John, Curly-Headed Doctor, and others to meet in a tent at a neutral site on the Lava Beds.

Winema, a Modoc married to settler Frank Riddle, warned Canby and the others to expect trouble from Captain Jack and his band. But Canby ignored Winema's warning, perhaps assured that the Indians wouldn't dare try anything violent in the presence of more than 1,000 soldiers.

But he was wrong. Canby was murdered in an act of treachery usually blamed on Schonchin John and Curly-Headed Doctor, although Captain Jack reportedly went along with it. The Reverend Doctor Eleazer Thomas, a Methodist minister, was also killed. Frank Riddle, who acted as an interpreter, and L.S. Dyar escaped with Winema's help. She is also credited with saving the life of A.B. Meacham, an Indian agent who was shot seven times by Schonchin but lived because Winema kept spoiling the assassin's aim.

After the massacre, the Modocs were hunted down with a vengeance by federal troops. Captain Jack and five of his followers, including Schonchin, were captured and hanged at Fort Klamath. Other tribal members were shipped to a reservation in Oklahoma.

The banishment of Indians to reservations and rancherias ended organized resistance to the settlers in Northern California, but animosities have continued to this day and occasionally surface in acts of discontent.

The west bank area of Shasta County, that eventually became Redding, remained remarkably clear of clashes involving Indians during the early years of the county's history.

There were probably several reasons for this quiet. For one, the Wintu occupied high ground, and were by nature occupied with peaceful pursuits. Wintu were also numerous and used to dealing from positions of strength. Tribal leaders seemed quite willing to deal with the newcomers on business terms. Also, they did not seek more territory like the aggressive Yana.

On the settlers' side, there appears to have been a general feeling of amity toward Indians among the civic leaders of old Shasta. For example, Dr. Benjamin Shurtleff, alcalde of Shasta under Mexican rule, treated the Indians without charge. To be sure, there were nuisance reports of Indians filching blankets from miners sleeping off rough work days and rowdy nights, and incidents of violence and violent retaliation. But Shasta was spared the excesses of bad Indian-white relations that occurred elsewhere, such as in Cottonwood and Millville.

A prevailing influence in maintaining what friendship there was lay in the genuine paternal concern of Shasta County's first resident. Born November 26, 1816, in New Jersey, Pierson Barton Reading left home at the age of fourteen to seek his fortune in the South. He became a cotton broker in Vicksburg, Mississippi, and later a New Orleans merchant.

He married and fathered a daughter, Jeanette, but his young wife died and a business partner absconded, leaving him bankrupt and $60,000 in debt. Saddened by his losses, Reading left his daughter in a New Orleans convent and migrated to the West. He and Samuel Hensley, a banker friend, joined the Chiles-Walker party bound for California in May 1843 near Independence, Missouri, a contingent that included nearly 1,000 emigrants and 100 wagons.

The party overcame the trail hazards of Indian strife, stormy weather, sickness, food shortages, and dissension, arriving in October at Fort Hall, in what is now Idaho.

Chiles-Walker leaders then sent a party of thirteen men including Reading to Sutter's Fort to obtain supplies for the rest of the journey. Reaching Fort Boise by October, they blazed a new trail southward into California.

The party camped at the source of the Pit River, then traveled south along the river to enter the Sacramento Valley, reaching Sutter's Fort on November 9. Reading then became a clerk and chief trapper for Sutter while Hensley returned to what is now Shasta County to cut timber and send logs downriver to the fort.

Reading became so valuable to Sutter that the Swiss pioneer once left him in charge of the fort while Sutter helped Mexican Governor Manuel Micheltorena put down a military rebellion in the south.

In May 1845 at Sutter's request, Reading led a trapping expedition north to map a route into present Trinity County and, along the way, collect a disputed debt from the irascible Peter Lassen, a famous trailblazer and an early resident of Shasta. Reading trapped beaver and otter in waters of the north state and Oregon, and with a party of thirty men and 100 horses crossed the mountains near Backbone Ridge, now between Redding and Shasta Lake, and went westward into Trinity County. Reading named the Trinity River under the mistaken impression that it emptied into Trinidad Bay on the Pacific Ocean.

In 1846 Reading played a prominent role in the Bear Flag Revolt, helping to draw up plans for a "Bear Flag Party" with William Ide of Red Bluff, keeping records in a laudatory manner, and later helping to write a peace treaty.

Reading and Frémont, a key figure in the revolt, apparently got along well together. He enlisted in Frémont's battalion in July 1846 and left on a ship for San Diego with the pathfinder, his staff, and about 300 men. Reading was appointed paymaster for all U.S. troops in California with the rank of major and did his work so scrupulously he was later commended by the federal government for it.

Reading's restless nature and yen for adventure sometimes forced others to tend to his problems. A Frenchman named Julian was left to watch Reading's adobe rancho—which he gave the flamboyant name Rancho Buena Ventura—in the summer of 1845. Julian was either chased away or killed by Indians who burned the house and ran off livestock while Reading spent ten days roaming his Buena Ventura grant. In 1847 Reading built a second house, restocked the land, and planted fruit trees and the first grapevines north of New Helvetia (Sutter's native Swiss name for his lands).

But problems on the homefront couldn't settle him down. Reading was among the first to visit Marshall's mill at Coloma. Intrigued by the gold discovery in the millrace and the imminent discovery of gold at Reading Springs, he outfitted an expedition that included three whites and sixty-nine Indians to prospect on the Trinity River. The expedition found gold at Reading's Bar. Reading was able to take out $80,000 in gold dust before abandoning the claim six weeks later, retreating from an encounter with some unfriendly Oregonians.

Reading went to Washington, D.C., in 1850 to complete his accounting as paymaster and pay off $60,000 in debts remaining from the 1837 bankruptcy. He made a second trip to the capital in 1855. While there, he met and married Fannie Wallace Washington, a distant relative of the nation's first president, and brought her to Rancho Buena Ventura.

Reading almost became the state's governor in 1851, losing to John Bigler by only a few hundred votes. He learned later that he might have won: a man confessed to Reading that he had deliberately destroyed 1,000 votes which would have elected the major.

That same year Reading fared better when he was unhorsed by a dying grizzly bear he had shot while hunting. A blow from the bear threw Reading's horse on him, breaking his leg, but inflicting no further injury on the major as he lay all night listening to the bear crashing around in the underbrush.

Reading had built a mansion adjoining the adobe in 1853, and after that enjoyed for several years the fruits of his labors. The original adobe became one of the homes for his vaqueros. Reading's ranchhouse soon became known for its hospitality in much the way Sutter's Fort had become a stopping place in future Sacramento.

Reading died in May 1868 at the age of fifty-one, leaving a widow and five children. Lawsuits and mortgages withered away his estate, depriving his descendants of their inheritance.

A fire destroyed Reading's mansion and burned to the south wall of the adobe. The remaining structure, after standing for almost a century, eventually fell victim to vandalism and the elements. Fort Reading was also destroyed by one of the county's many brushfires.

A replica of Reading's adobe houses the Shasta College Museum while the original site marks the entrance to Reading Island, a recreation area. The island is one of the few places that bear the name of Redding's first and foremost settler, who almost had a town named after him.

Pierson B. Reading is known as the "Father of Shasta County." The first permanent settler in the county, Reading migrated to the West in 1843 where he worked for John Sutter as a clerk and then a trapper along the upper portion of the Sacramento River. Courtesy, Shasta State Historic Park Courthouse Museum

The Rush for Riches

News of the gold strikes in Northern California spread on the wind, drawing adventurers by the thousands. Men of all ages, some with wives, came to live in shanties, tents, and bedrolls under the stars, staking life savings and even life itself on finding enough yellow flakes and nuggets to make the effort worthwhile.

Miners and would-be miners came to the north state in a human flood that lasted almost a decade. Sailors deserted their ships in the harbor at San Francisco, paying for passage with their labor. Travelers relayed the information to East Coast newspapers and fired the imaginations of young men, from roustabouts to college students.

Wooden vessels plying the trade winds around Cape Horn groaned and creaked with their extra passengers. Bonfires twinkled like low stars on the prairies as wayfarers in wagon trains rested between long days on overland trails westward to the gold country. Soon the freight roads north of Sacramento were teeming with travelers, many on freshly bought horses and mules, all eager to be first at the diggings and strike it rich.

Major Reading was caught up in the rush for riches long enough to square his debts, take a much-desired trip to his boyhood home on the East Coast, and acquire a second wife. After that, he turned more to the agrarian life of Rancho Buena Ventura.

Others, like Reading, foresook the muddy streams of uncertain riches for the more durable streams of commerce. They established stores, hotels, saloons, commission houses, lumberyards, and livery stables—the building blocks of security.

The Deadwood Mine in Trinity County, shown here circa 1900, used steam-powered machinery which raised heavy iron "stamps" several inches, then dropped them to crush the ore passing beneath. The pulverized ore, mixed with water, was then washed over a mercury-coated surface which separated the gold from the ore. Stamp mills were in common operation into the early 1900s. Courtesy, Shasta State Historic Park Courthouse Museum

Small communities sprang up overnight, some existing but briefly until gold strikes waned and townsfolk drifted away, their buildings lost to fire, scavenging, and neglect. As placer mining dwindled, the old gold towns faded. Nothing much remains of such frontier communities as Horsetown, Middletown, Kettlebelly, Muletown, Churntown, Briggsville, and Texas Springs, their sites all now on the periphery of present-day Redding. A few still have inhabitants on a reduced scale. Centerville lives on as a community services district, Buckeye as a school district, and French Gulch as a tiny historic town with a century-old hotel. Once flourishing settlements southeast of Redding, Piety Hill and Eagle Creek also declined, to be revived later as diminutive Igo and Ono.

Redding was actually born independently of this Gold Rush. Unlike the other frontier communities which grew around a water hole or a crossing of trails, Redding began as a planned community. The city was incorporated in 1887, but actually got its start fifteen years earlier.

B.B. Redding, the town's namesake, sent a survey crew to the Redding area, then called Poverty Flat, to lay out a townsite in 1872. By this time, all that was left of the rush of Forty-Niners were a few campgrounds for teamsters at Reid's Ferry beside the Sacramento where the city's venerable Diestelhorst Bridge is today. There had been an Indian village (near where the county's Justice Center now stands at the intersection of West and Placer streets), but even that was gone by 1872.

Redding hoped the new town would serve as a railhead for the Central Pacific Railroad pushing north from Red Bluff. A land agent for the Southern Pacific Railroad and its subsidiary the Central Pacific until his death in 1882, Redding also had a distinguished record in public service.

Born in Nova Scotia, Redding came West in 1849 to prospect, but instead became involved with politics in Sacramento, where he served as mayor in 1856. From 1863 to 1867 Redding was California's secretary of state. He was also a conservationist and student of wildlife, writing numerous articles on subjects ranging from fish culture to the Galapagos Islands. He is credited with organizing the State Board of Fish Commissioners, forerunner of the state Fish and Game Commission. As a member of the board from 1874 to 1882, whenever Redding went by rail into the north state his train usually

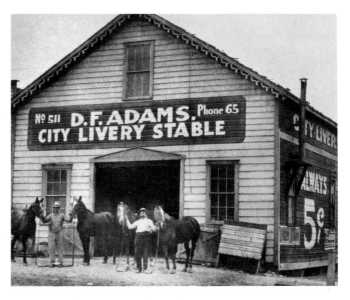

Above: *The City Livery Stable, owned by D.F. Adams, shown here in the early 1900s, was situated on the south side of Placer, west of California Street and east of the railroad tracks. Livery stables were a common necessity in the days before the automobile. Not every city dweller owned horses or buggies so they were rented from the neighborhood livery stable. Courtesy, Maida Glover Gandy*

Opposite page, top: *The Trinity Centre Hotel was a favorite stopping place for miners and other early travelers in the mid and late 1800s. Trinity Centre was on the road over the Shasta-Trinity Divide from the towns of Whiskeytown and Shasta. Courtesy, Shasta State Historic Park Courthouse Museum*

Opposite page, bottom: *Harrison Gulch was one of many mining towns that sprang up around Redding. Two miners panning in the creek that flows through the gulch discovered gold in 1893. The place was named after W.R. Harrison, elected in 1850 as the first judge in Shasta County. By the early 1900s, when this picture was taken, the town had faded and was no longer a bustling community. Courtesy, Charlotte Engle*

Above: *From the early 1850s until the Diestelhorst Bridge was built in 1915, Reid's Ferry was in continuous operation at the point where the bridge crosses the Sacramento River today. Ferries were common and essential in the years of horse-and-wagon travel as well as in the early days of automobile transportation. Courtesy, Shasta Historical Society*

included a tank car loaded with fish for transplanting in lakes and streams along the way.

The foreman of the survey crew proudly named the townsite "Redding," after his enterprising boss. In doing so, he ignored Redding's first settler, Major Piersen B. Reading. Reading's fans did try to preserve his name for the new community, yet confusion existed from the start in newspapers of the time, with some spelling the new town's name as "Redding" and others stubbornly calling it "Reading." The naming wasn't accomplished without heated squabbles that were eventually decided in the state legislature.

(Ironically, the first name of Shasta was Reading Springs. In his luckless bouts with history, Major Reading again couldn't make his name stick.)

Shasta, the county's first community, nestled in the red clay foothills six miles west of Redding, was born in a blaze of gold dust and glory in 1848. Once a mere stopover for teamsters freighting goods to settlers in the mountains, Shasta became a brawling frontier town overnight with all the necessities required of hungry miners and their gold.

Other sleepy communities where previously a stranger was conversation for a day also blossomed overnight with immigrants. French Gulch, a hamlet fourteen

miles west of present Redding on the foot trails to the Trinities and Oregon, thrived on the influx of miners and freight handlers. A man named Feeney built a saloon there that later became the historic French Gulch Hotel, which celebrated its 100th anniversary in 1985.

In between Shasta and French Gulch lay a community that no longer exists, but had a name which has become world-famous: Whiskeytown. A one-street town similar to others in the Old West, its site lies forever beneath the waters of man-made Whiskeytown Lake.

No one knows quite how the town got its name, but the prevailing legend is that a mule laden with kegs of whiskey stumbled and lost its cargo, to the delight of thirsty miners nearby. The creek was immediately christened Whiskey Creek and the name stuck.

At one time Whiskeytown was a thriving freight stop between Shasta and the mining camps of Trinity and Siskiyou counties. The community existed until the early 1960s, when most of its buildings, sagging with age, were torn down to make way for Whiskeytown Lake. A store and post office were transplanted on Whiskey Creek, where old-time residents hold a lakeshore reunion every year.

Whiskeytown and French Gulch, like Shasta, served a dual purpose. They were communities for the drift-

Above: *Whisky Town (later spelled Whiskeytown) grew up around mining. Most of the larger mines in the Redding area were built with money derived from the sale of stock to investors who hoped to reap huge dividends from their investments when the mines struck the elusive paydirt. Many were rewarded, but many others were not. Courtesy, Shasta State Historic Park Courthouse Museum*

Above, left: *B.B. Redding, a land agent for the Southern Pacific Railroad, is the person for whom the town was named. A native of Nova Scotia, he died in August of 1882, soon after this photograph was taken, having paid only one visit to the town bearing his name. Courtesy, Shasta Historical Society*

Opposite page: *This circa 1900 photograph shows horse and wagon activity along Main Street in French Gulch, about twenty-five miles west of Redding. With the coming of the railroad to Redding, wagon roads that led out of the new railhead city were more frequently traveled with freight wagons, stagecoaches, and buggy traffic. Courtesy, Shasta State Historic Park Courthouse Museum*

wood mining population and a freight depot for the mule trains that brought supplies to goldseekers in streamside tent and shack villages in the Trinity and Siskiyou mountains beyond.

Dubbed by its boosters as the "Queen City of the North," Shasta was by far the most prosperous of the three. Shasta was also the junction where freight wagons from the south transferred their cargoes to muleback for the hazardous narrow trails ahead.

At the time of the Gold Rush, Shasta was a key community on the pioneer route to Yreka and Oregon. Freight wagons later rolled up an easier route through the Sacramento River Canyon but by then the community and the Gold Rush which inspired it were on the wane. The boomtown lost more prominence when railroad builders decided to plant tracks up the Sacramento River Canyon to the east and chose Redding as the site for their railhead.

Shasta's importance was eclipsed completely after mining companies discovered massive copper-bearing ore deposits and established smelters at Keswick, Kennett, Coram, Bully Hill, and Ingot. Meanwhile, the railroad was pushed northward up the Sacramento River Canyon, reaching as far as Delta—now near the north shore of Shasta Lake—in 1884 and then to Dunsmuir, fifty-two miles north of Redding, in 1886.

Eventually Dunsmuir became the division capital of the Southern Pacific for the north state and remained so until recent decades when automation and attrition centralized railroad operations at Gerber.

Before Shasta's decline, it had flourished during the 1850s despite severe fires, bankruptcies, and other hazards.

The city also produced a remarkable collection of civic leaders, men like Isaac Roop, the town's first postmaster; Chauncey Carroll "C.C." Bush, who later became Redding's first mayor; and Dr. Benjamin Shurtleff, alcalde of Shasta under Mexican rule.

Born July 31, 1831, in Pittsfield, Massachusetts, Bush came West in 1850 from St. Joseph, Missouri, reaching Shasta in February 1851. Scarcely old enough to grow the flowing white beard he sported in later life, Bush first tried muleback freight packing from Shasta to Yreka. Later he turned to mining for several years in the Churntown and Buckeye districts. He eventually opened a store in Shasta, and was the first merchant to open a large store in Redding.

Roop's prominence came when he moved to the

Honey Lake Valley near Susanville and became involved in a territorial dispute known locally as Roop's War. He was one of the principals in a futile movement to gain recognition of an independent "State of Nataqua" between California and Nevada.

Since only about one-third of the prospectors claimed their mail (the *Shasta Courier* regularly ran lists of addresses), Roop's duties as postmaster were probably light. He spent more time mining his claim at Whiskey Creek. Later he ran a store at Oak Bottom, now a marina of Whiskeytown Lake.

Shurtleff was a diamond in the rough. A descendant of the Pilgrims and Harvard educated, he received his medical degree in 1848, then heard of the gold strike in California and came West, reaching San Francisco on July 6, 1849. He was working for miners in Placer County when he heard about the gold discoveries near Shasta.

Shasta provided a fertile field for the imagination of the young doctor, who had been a pupil of Oliver Wendell Holmes. In a short time he was elected alcalde with the judicial power to try any case. He began practicing medicine, opened a drugstore, and went into the mercantile business. He also obtained an interest in brick manufacture.

Shurtleff returned to Massachusetts in 1852, married Ann Griffith of Wareham, and returned with her by boat and muleback via the Isthmus of Panama (his first trip had been entirely by schooner around Cape Horn). They raised three sons, including Benjamin Shurtleff who went on to become county treasurer, state senator, and eventually director of the Napa state asylum (now the Napa State Hospital).

But fame is fleeting. Despite all his public works, Shurtleff is best remembered for his hilltop mansion, which hugged a brush-covered hill overlooking the town from the west.

He began building it in the summer of 1851. By his own measure it was forty-two-feet long and twenty-two-feet wide. Floors were made of white pine lumber shipped around Cape Horn. The yellow pine timbers were hand-hewn locally, including ground sills and sleepers, from trees in nearby forests. The framing lumber was whipsawed by local millers whose sawmill operated on horsepower, earning them as much as $1,000 per thousand board feet.

After Shasta nearly was reduced to ashes by the fire of June 14, 1853, Western Star Lodge 2 of the Masonic

Above: *The town of Shasta, shown here sometime between 1860 and 1875, became the county seat in February 1851. The Empire Hotel is on the left with the courthouse on its right. The first two-story building beyond the courthouse is the Masonic Lodge, California's first, brought here in 1851 by Peter Lassen. As the trailhead for supply shipments to the mines of Trinity and Siskiyou counties, it flourished at a mad pace. But by 1860 new roads had been built into the mining country and in 1862 Shasta's population dropped to 2,000. Courtesy, Shasta State Historic Park Courthouse Museum*

Left: *Chauncey Carroll Bush was the first merchant to come to Redding. His driving enthusiasm and business and civic leadership earned him the title of "Father of Redding." When the town of Redding was established, Bush was the first to open a business. He served as the city's first mayor and as the county's judge. Courtesy, Shasta Historical Society*

Lodge met in an unfinished hall of the house until suitable quarters could be found. Shurtleff's wife left the house on manufactured errands during the Masons' afternoon meetings so as not to intrude on their mystic rites.

The lodge, the first grand lodge to be chartered in California, is a story in itself. It was chartered through the efforts of Peter Lassen, a Tehama County rancher who managed to have its charter brought safely by wagon train from Missouri, according to most accounts.

Lassen has been described as headstrong, unpredictable, and nomadic. Yet he had the courage to lead wagon trains across trackless wasteland and the ability to inspire pioneers to follow him.

Perhaps as many as 100,000 immigrants braved great hardship to cross the Great Plains, the Rockies, and the Sierra to reach California during the Gold Rush. As many as 50,000 people made the trek with 100,000 livestock in 1852 alone. Many followed the Lassen Trail.

The immigrants traveled in everything from farm wagons to heavy freight vehicles and bulky, canvas-topped Conestogas pulled by mules, oxen, or horses. Usually two wagons were used, one to carry family belongings and supplies.

Shasta welcomed the immigrants. One newcomer, Solomon Kingery, was wined and dined in style at the St. Charles Hotel for being among the first to arrive by the Nobles' Trail. It was a bad move for Kingery, who arrived in Shasta August 22, 1855, and died there three summers later at age twenty-five.

Meanwhile, the town grew. Figures vary but it is safe to say that several thousand goldseekers swarmed into nearby streams and rivulets, while several hundred became actual residents of Shasta, Middletown, Horsetown, and other such communities.

Some clung like gold dust to a pan, and prospered. Businesses like Bull, Baker and Company exchanged needed household goods for gold in transactions with miners from the creeks. The store in Shasta soon became parent to a flour mill in Red Bluff.

Relationships among the new settlers, miners, and storekeepers, not to mention the host Indians, were often strained, to say the least. Alpheus Bull, in a June 7, 1850 letter to his sister, wrote "the Indians have stolen a great number of mules, oxen and horses. The whites have instigated them by their base conduct toward the Indians."

Opposite page: *Samson, shown here circa 1910, was an Indian caught between two cultures. His family and tribal ancestors lived in the Slate Creek area near LaMoine. His name was earned when he packed a 190-pound anvil from Delta to the Trinity County mines. At seventy years of age he could outrun all challengers: when running he would place his manzanita cane behind his back and lock it inside his elbows. Samson died in June 1916. Courtesy, Shasta Historical Society*

Left: *Charles Litsch, leaning against the counter on the right, was proprietor of the Litsch general store in Shasta in 1893 when this photograph was taken. The Litsch store is a landmark from a bygone era. Operated continuously by the Litsch family until the 1960s, the store has now been completely restored as a "living museum" with the shelves and showcases stocked just as they were originally. Courtesy, Shasta State Historic Park Courthouse Museum*

There was also streamside rivalry among the Western immigrants, most of whom had earlier mining experience, and the "Eastern greenhorns" who ventured West as fortune seekers. Many of the early arrivals that swelled Horsetown's population to upwards of 400 were "generally churlish and selfish" with the newcomers, according to B.F. Frank and H.W. Chappell in an 1881 county publication.

Devastating fires almost wiped out Shasta's business district on two occasions, the second causing townspeople to rebuild with brick on a main street that was 100 feet wide. But another fire swept the town several years later and Shasta was all but abandoned.

Shasta's decline in the 1880s coincided with the rise of Redding. After the courthouse was wrested from Shasta in 1888, it was all over for the Queen City, but the memories linger. Several history-oriented organizations in recent years have attempted to restore the old Litsch store and other buildings that have formed Shasta's ruin, now a state historical park. An interpretive group has begun staging dramatizations of historic events. The main attraction, however, still is the old former courthouse, carefully restored as a state monument. Trials of the Ono Justice Court were held

there regularly until the retirement of Judge Glen W. Knudson several years ago. It is still used for special occasions like weddings.

Prisoners waited for freedom or eternity in small, dark cells in the courthouse basement. In 1859 poet Joaquin Miller spent time in an earlier jail in Shasta, escaping, so it is said, with the help of his lover, an Indian woman. Miller later insisted his arrest was a misunderstanding, that he was accused of horse stealing when the animal in question was a mule.

While some did find riches, for many who pulled stakes and came to California to seek their fortune, the Gold Rush was a miserable experience. It meant long hours of back-breaking work, bent over in midstream squinting into a gold pan under a burning sun, hoping to find specks of gold.

Life in the mining camp wasn't much to write home about, either. A miner's diet consisted of such staples as bacon, spuds, flour (usually sourdough), dried fruits in season, and fresh meat and vegetables when they were available. Few took the trouble to plant gardens, and hunting elusive deer meant taking valuable time away from claims.

Many weren't prepared for the rigors of frontier life.

Above: *The miner in this circa 1875 photograph is standing next to a flume—an important device in early hydraulic or placer mining. Long wooden flumes carried water great distances to the remote mining locations where hydraulic monitors were set up. The flume also allowed the water to gain speed and momentum for increased pressure at the mine site. Courtesy, Roberta Martin and the Shasta Historical Society*

Top: *The Royal T. Sprague Mine near Shasta, shown here circa 1880, is representative of many such mines laboriously dug by hardrock miners who followed their intuitions and searched beneath the ground for gold. When streams dried up during the hot summer months, miners set aside their pans and sluiceboxes and bored into the earth. Courtesy, Shasta State Historic Park Courthouse Museum*

The former clerks, farmers, students, and drifters often were unsuited for the frustrating work of separating ounces of gold from acres of sand and gravel. Many became sick and some died of mysterious illnesses like the "bloody flux." Some were murdered in their bedrolls or died in bitter brawls over mining rights. The majority either gave up after discouraging results or used their earnings to establish farms or stores.

For those who chose to stay streamside, miners could claim stream frontages from twelve to sixty feet, depending on local miner's law. There was no limit on how far back a claim could go, and prospectors would claim vast strips of land uphill from the stream.

When the streambeds yielded fewer specks and nuggets, many miners turned to "hardrock diggings," using small, short-handled shovels or kitchen utensils to burrow into the hillsides. The first mines were little more than warrens that the Forty-Niners called "dog holes" or "coyote holes." As the mines deepened, timbers were added for support and miners carried lighted candles to work by and to detect the presence of harmful gases. The early mines were seldom braced well and some became tombs for their hapless owners.

When heavy rains occurred, as in October 1849, the eager prospectors waded into the flooding gulches with gold pans at the ready. Some made as much as $100 per day, no mean profit in those days.

In the late 1850s and early 1860s, as surface gold became scarce, more sophisticated mining methods were used. Chinese immigrants, using methods developed for terraced agriculture in their homeland, built elaborate networks of ditches and wooden flumes to carry water from upper-elevation springs to their diggings. Other miners followed suit, organizing companies that supplied irrigation water to farmers as well as to miners for their sluiceboxes. A "miner's inch" is still used as a unit of measure for delivery of irrigation water via the old ditch-side systems.

Other early-day mining methods gave way to hydraulic monitors called "giants," great cannon-like devices that shaved away hillsides with a water force that could knock a man senseless. The water cannons turned streams into slag heaps of gravel and created such environmental havoc that public pressure caused them to be outlawed by the state legislature.

But by that time mining had gone underground. Mines like the Washington at French Gulch were drawing expertise from as far away as Wales. Explora-

*With the decline in abundance of surface gold, miners began using
other methods to uncover the metal. Placer mining, which involved
the use of hydraulic nozzles called "monitors," was a popular way to
erode the soil and wash it through sluiceboxes to obtain the elusive
gold. This form of mining left vast scars on the landscape and eventually became unpopular. Courtesy, Shasta State Historic Park
Courthouse Museum*

The Bully Hill smelter, shown here circa 1909, was located where Horse and Squaw creeks enter the Pit River. Gold was first discovered there in 1853. Silver, zinc, and copper were also mined, until 1927, the last year of major production at the Bully Hill mine. Courtesy, Shasta Historical Society

tion was financed by major financial interests.

While the railhead town of Redding missed the streamside binge of the Gold Rush, it was well positioned for the underground mining boom.

Early discoveries by Charles Camden, James Sallee, and Colonel William Magee confirmed the existence of a mass sulfide deposit that began with Iron Mountain approximately ten miles northwest of Redding and extended for several miles along the west side of the Sacramento River Canyon into what is now Shasta Lake. Among the first companies to realize the potential of the area was the Mountain Copper Company of London, England, which absorbed earlier companies and began mining on Iron Mountain as the 1800s ended.

Although the fan-shaped formation of ore-bearing rock northwest to northeast of Redding was called a "golden crescent," the real draw was copper. Extracting the ore meant digging several tunnels with a central vertical connecting shaft along which ore, men, and equipment were moved. Lateral tunnels called "adits" also reached the interiors with narrow-gauge railways. It was hard, dangerous work, but for many it was the only work available during Redding's early years of development.

From 1896 to 1919, copper was a basic resource of the Shasta County economy, drawn from a network of

Above: *Slim Warren's famous mahogany bar at the Diamond Hotel in Kennett was known as the best saloon for miles around. The ornate, hand-carved bar, majestic columns, grape-cluster electric lights, and burly brass cash register made the place an oasis of elegance in a rough and rowdy community. Courtesy, Bureau of Reclamation, Shasta Dam*

Above, left: *The riches of the Iron Mountain Mine were first discovered in the 1860s by a U.S. land surveyor named Magee. About 1890 a twenty-stamp mill was built on the mountain for pounding ore to dust in the search for silver. In 1897 the silver mill was destroyed by fire. Although the fire was a setback, the mine was quickly rebuilt and production continued. It is not known if this photo was taken before or after the fire, but it is among the earliest known views of the operation. Courtesy, Shasta Historical Society*

ridges that also produced zinc, cadmium, lead, and sulfur in addition to limestone and acidic compounds. Needed for automobiles, telephone and electric wires, and other industrial uses of a dawning era, copper nurtured the boom-and-bust communities of Keswick, Coram, Kennett, Bully Hill, Copper City, De La Mar, Winthrop and Ingot, all within the "crescent" and some whose past is forever lost to the waters of the lake. Only Keswick and Ingot still have inhabitants.

The five major copper mines at the turn of the century were the Iron Mountain at Keswick (which was the area's major employer during the Depression), the Bully Hill on the Pit River near Copper City, the Afterthought at Ingot, the Mammoth at Kennett, and the Balaklala at Coram.

Kennett and Coram particularly thrived during the copper mining boom. Kennett, like the city of Redding, was actually laid out as a railroad townsite in 1884. The town was named for a railroad worker named Kennet, but the name was misspelled by a mapmaker.

At its peak of prosperity, Kennett had 5,000 residents. The mining town became famous for a tavern—Slim Warren's Diamond Bar Saloon—said at the time to be the fanciest drinking spot between Portland and San Francisco.

Besides the Diamond Bar, there were twelve other saloons, a newspaper, a two-story opera house, and a quarter-of-a-mile of red-light district. Kennett also had the copper smelter of Mammoth Copper Company, a smelter capable of spewing forth fumes that could kill orchards in Happy Valley, fifteen miles away.

Kennett disappeared forever when Shasta Lake was filled. Downstream one-and-a-half miles from Shasta Dam, the site of old Coram still exists, but only as a

Above: *In its prime, Kennett was a roaring town. Today the site that 5,000 people called home is deep beneath the waters of Shasta Lake. This 1905 photo shows a portion of the railroad along which Kennett was started in 1884. The Diamond Hotel, housing Slim Warren's legendary Diamond Bar & Saloon, appears in the lower left corner. Courtesy, Maida Glover Gandy*

Right: *Though Kennett was laid out along the railroad tracks, the surrounding terrain was anything but level, as this 1905 view shows. The town's booming growth at the turn of the century slowed considerably and by 1930 Kennett was virtually abandoned and in ruins. Courtesy, Maida Glover Gandy*

part of history.

Named for a mining man from Montana, Coram was started in 1906 as a mining community for the Balaklala Copper Company, which took copper, silver, iron, and silica from its holdings. Coram once boasted twenty-three saloons where the hard drinkers among some 160 miners could clear their sinuses of smelter fumes on weeknights, while saving their real binges for Saturday nights in Redding. Coram also held twelve rooming houses, three hotels, and two butcher shops.

During its heyday the Balaklala Mine produced 1,000 tons of ore a day, which was spirited by aerial tramway to a smelter three miles away. Upwards of 500 men were employed in Coram mining operations.

But owners of Coram's noxious smelter bowed to public demand and closed it down in 1911 because of air pollution. Skidding copper prices did the rest. By 1918 the town was the smallest incorporated community in the United States with thirty recorded residents. Coram briefly made news in 1977 when fourteen parcels of the original townsite were sold at auction, mostly to local history buffs.

Mining activity became dormant early in the century until it was revived by the demand for copper during World War I. Most of the mines had closed for good by the late 1920s but some managed to linger in production.

One, the Reid Mine near Buckeye, was revived in 1983 with exploratory testing for gold by a complex of interests based in Vancouver, British Columbia. Temporarily halted for several months by litigation, work was resumed in 1985.

Another, Iron Mountain, remained inactive from 1963 until late 1985, when present owners T.W. Arman and Frank Foster of Sacramento teamed up with the prestigious Davy McKee engineering corporation of San Francisco in a plan to extract minerals by in situ (solution) mining of the tunnels. Their $30-million plan, contingent upon approval of state and federal environmental agencies, was still in limbo as of June 1986.

Ingot, east of Redding on Highway 299, once provided a community for the Afterthought Mine, which can still be seen as a ruin by the highway. Operated sporadically for ninety years, the Afterthought disgorged its hoard of copper, lead, silver, zinc, and gold to a succession of owners until it was closed for good in 1952.

The site of De La Mar, a town that provided twelve saloons, several brothels, a school, and a church for workers of the Bully Hill Mine, can be reached by boat on Shasta Lake. All that remains are a stone hydroelectric powerhouse, and winery and smelter ruins. The rest of the abandoned town was burned years ago. Copper City, another town near the Bully Hill mine, now exists only in the memories of those who grew up there.

A historical marker in south Redding recalls the existence of Horsetown, which grew to 1,000 inhabitants on Clear Creek approximately where it is crossed by Highway 273. Horsetown grew from a mining camp started by Major Reading, who set his Indian ranch workers to look for gold in Clear Creek after John Marshall's discovery of nuggets in Coloma.

Stories vary about Horsetown's name. One version is that a traveler with a two-horse team and wagon was stopped in town when one horse fell dead. Rebuffed when he tried to buy another, the traveler angrily called it a "one-horse town."

At its peak, Horsetown had two hotels, numerous shops and stores, a Catholic church, fourteen saloons, and a newspaper, *The Northern Argus*, established in 1857. When the rush for gold waned, so did Horsetown. One night in 1868 it was swept away by a fire that took most of its buildings.

Although they provided paychecks for thousands of workmen and economic benefits for several communities, the early-day mines proved detrimental to the environment. The blighted landscape left by smelters drew the wrath of orchardists and other concerned citizens, who demanded closure of the smelters. One mine—Iron Mountain—left a legacy of water pollution problems from copper slag heaps that are still plaguing users and intriguing engineers.

Though the mining industry caused numerous problems, the mines also produced wealth during those early years. Total value of mining production reached $11.5 million annually, according to some accounts.

And though the boom was followed by bust, mining brought several decades of prosperity that knitted together the social, political, and economic elements of the growing community. It made Redding viable enough to attempt the grand adventure that was to make it the north state's water conservation capital and undisputed hub of outdoor recreation: the building of Shasta Dam.

Progress
at Poverty Flat

ne can imagine what kind of start Redding had as a community on August 3, 1872.

It was no doubt a hot, dusty, summer day. A motley gang of railroad workers sleeved away the sweat and grime as they squinted up the tracks, straining to see the special train that was bringing railroad dignitaries and potential land buyers. In the distance a smoke column appeared and grew closer with the sound of chugging and the long, mournful wail of a locomotive whistle.

Among the railroad workers were many Chinese, who were alternately praised and spurned for their hard work and tenacity in Shasta County as elsewhere on the frontier. Indians astride bareback calmed their nervous horses. Miners taking a holiday from their diggings thronged the destination point. Shasta's social and business elite sat in their buggies, and farmers leaned against wagons, waiting for the big event. Cowhands hunkered in weather-beaten saddles on rangy steeds.

The train's passengers, undeterred by a joyful greeting of gunshots, hats-in-air shouts, and fanfare from the inevitable cornet band, kicked at the clods, squinted at the burning sun, and shook their heads. A town here? Appalling!

So, despite no-doubt soaring rhetoric from the top Central Pacific officials, including no less than Mark Hopkins and B.R. Crocker, only seventeen of the hundred lots that James B. Haggin wrested from an in-

Workers shown here in 1888 take a break from their labors to pose on the nearly completed Bank of Northern California on the southeast corner of Market and Yuba streets. With the railroad running parallel to it just two blocks to the west, Market Street became a main artery in the downtown area. Courtesy, Shasta Historical Society

Edward Frisbie was a banker who believed in the future of Redding right from its conception. In 1872, when the Central Pacific Railroad offered 100 lots in Redding for sale, Frisbie bought eighty-three. Within a month he resold the land, and the railhead city was off to a good start. Courtesy, Shasta Historical Society

debted Major Reading moved under the auctioneer's gavel that summer day. (The major, who died in 1868, had mortgaged part of Rancho Buena Ventura to Hensley to cover his losses in an ill-fated navigational venture and Fannie Reading, his widow, was unable to show the debt had been paid.)

The *Shasta Courier* reported that the highest bid was $160 and the total amount reached $1,500, with all but three sales going to local residents, adding caustically, "the bars took in more money that day."

The remaining lots were bought by a daring pioneer banker, Edward Frisbie—a man who knew a good deal when he saw one. Frisbie's judgment proved sound; within a month all 100 lots were sold.

Redding's business district at that time was about seven blocks in all. Its outermost streets formed the perimeter of the original town and had such "original" names as North (now Eureka Way), South, East, and West. The Redding Hotel, a depot hostelry, was the first commercial building erected, according to most accounts. The city's population was approximately 300.

C.C. Bush didn't waste any time settling into the new community. He immediately set to work building Redding's first large house. This dynamic ex-miner turned businessman brought New England business sense and Yankee daring in much-needed amounts to the struggling little community.

Historian Edward Petersen has called Bush the "father of Redding." He was everywhere. When the newly formed Hook and Ladder Company needed a foreman in 1879, Bush was their man. A newspaper editorial of the time stated, "Bush and push laid the foundation of the city . . . and Bush provided much of the push."

Undoubtedly, the community prospered despite almost constant sniping in its formative years by the *Shasta Courier*'s irascible editor, W.O. Carter, who also on occasion called for the extermination of Indians, Chinese, and anyone else who aroused his temper. Indeed, early accounts of Redding were anything but flattering and really didn't need Carter's attacks. Hogs roamed the streets, begging an ordinance to curb their wandering. Mudholes in winter gave way to potholes in summer. Rodents prospered from a lack of garbage collection. Such inconveniences were permissible for a temporary railhead, but intolerable in a growing city.

When the railroad moved north to plant railheads in Delta and Dunsmuir, Redding showed no signs of blowing away with the next dust devil off the prairie. These signs of permanence continued even after the devastating fires in 1874 and 1879, each of which almost wiped out the town's main business section.

There were several reasons for the city's longevity. When the railroad created Redding, the city became the terminus of freight and stagecoach lines that ran north, east, and west to mining camps and such communities as Weaverville, Burney, Fall River Mills, Millville, and Shingletown. Furthermore, the military's campaign against Captain Jack's Modoc warriors meant storing quartermaster supplies in Redding until they were needed in the north during the Lava Beds and Lost River campaigns of 1872 to 1873.

Fire, the nemesis of all frontier towns, in some ways proved to help the city's growth. When stores burned down in outlying communities, their owners sometimes relocated in Redding. Such was the case after a fire in Shasta had gutted even the new brick buildings.

Although Redding had its share of fires, residents seemed better organized to cope with them. Late one Saturday night in 1881, four patrons of a saloon rang fire bells and set off train whistles to warn the city of a growing blaze. The entire populace surrounded a city block and fought the fire to a standstill with pumper and hose cart, damp blankets, rugs, and a bucket brigade. They celebrated afterward with sandwiches, tea, and stronger liquid refreshments; the town was saved.

Bush and others on Redding's five-member board of trustees saw beyond the immediate hardships and perceived a city on the rise. But progress was slow. Almost fifteen years after the gavel fell on that first lot sale, in September 1887 Redding voters finally decided (205 to 103) to incorporate. The die was cast.

As each man glanced around the room at the others, the seriousness of the occasion must have weighed upon them.

To ease the transition of future officeholders, they drew lots for long and short (four-year and two-year) terms. Short terms were drawn by C.C. Bush and James McCormick, while long terms went to Jerry Culverhouse, J.F. Scamman, and W.W. Williams. With Bush as chairman, they took the oath of office as Redding's first board of trustees.

Bonds of $5,000 each were filled for city marshal and city treasurer, and $1,000 for city clerk. Sealed bids then were called for the first year's printing, to be presented at 7:00 p.m. on October 17. Regular meetings

Judge Chauncey Carroll Bush is shown here with his wife, Ida Schroeder Bush, circa 1890. Courtesy, Veronica Satorius

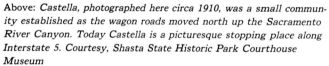

Above: *Castella, photographed here circa 1910, was a small community established as the wagon roads moved north up the Sacramento River Canyon. Today Castella is a picturesque stopping place along Interstate 5. Courtesy, Shasta State Historic Park Courthouse Museum*

Right, top: *On November 25, 1917, fire destroyed the Hotel Redding located on the southeast corner of Yuba and Oregon streets, site of the present post office. When first constructed, the hotel was called the Hotel Reading, but—reflecting the general confusion concerning the correct name for the city—the name above the arched doorway in this photograph is Hotel Redding. Courtesy, Maida Glover Gandy*

Above: *In 1912 the City of Redding bought a new Seagraves fire engine, the first motorized fire-fighting vehicle in Redding's history. Sitting at the wheel of the new rig is A.M. Dick with L.D. "Lou" Poole, fire chief, on the right. Courtesy, Ray and Rika Coffelt*

Left: *This is a photo of the North Star Mill in Millville as it appeared in 1890. Built on Cow Creek in 1855, the mill spawned a town second only to Shasta in population during the 1860s. Courtesy, Shasta State Historic Park Courthouse Museum*

As the railroad pushed further up the Sacramento River Canyon north of Redding, new communities were born. LaMoine, shown here in 1890, grew up around the tracks in a bend of the river. LaMoine was a sawmill town and also a mining base. Today LaMoine is little more than a freeway exit off Interstate 5. Courtesy, Shasta Historical Society

were scheduled monthly on the third Mondays.

The board then adjourned to October 12, a Wednesday, when it met to set salaries and adopt a code of ordinances. The meeting lasted until midnight.

The ordinances took effect November 1. Some were whimsical by today's standards but remarkably practical then. For example, the fiscal year began February 1, which allowed a month to settle accounts and update record books of the previous year. Trustees agreed to meet at 7:00 p.m. from October to May and 8:00 p.m. from June to September, not unlike Daylight Savings Time.

The town marshal was handed the lion's share of the work at a salary of twelve dollars per year, plus fines

and fees. For that he was required to keep law and order, act as fire marshal, and serve as the city's health officer. Who got the job is unclear, but it may have fallen to Bush, who doubled as justice of the peace and the city's first fire chief.

At that time the county's justice of the peace also acted as recorder, a job believed to have been also held by Bush. F.B. Simonds was appointed the first city recorder and M.A. Mitchell the first street superintendent at salaries of $2,000 each.

Mitchell, Scamman, and Ben Griffiths also were appointed fire wardens, while Drs. O.J. Lawry, J.H. Miller, J.W. McCoy, and B.E. Stevenson formed the city's first board of health.

The trustees also established Citizens Hook and Ladder Company No. 1 as Redding's first fire department. Residents using water for irrigation were required to shut off the faucet whenever the fire alarm sounded.

The marshal's duties included keeping women from entering "any saloon or public place where spiritous

The Shasta County Recorder's Office in 1898 was a busy place. The mining activity in the area was on the upswing with the large mines and smelters running full blast in search of copper, gold, silver, and zinc. Courtesy, Shasta Historical Society

malt or vinous liquors are sold" or "consorting with men, or playing at cards or games of chance."

The city's early laws also provided fines of five dollars to $100 for such offenses as "riding a horse, mule or other animal on a sidewalk except to cross it" and to ride or drive one in excess of ten miles per hour on any city street. And no person was allowed to discharge a firearm in town without written permission from the trustees.

Incorporation was not without its detractors, however. Shasta businessmen E. Lewin, John V. Scott, Henry Blumb, and A. Grotefend alleged in a full-page advertisement that the November 2, 1886, vote would lead to "political servility, boss rule and financial ruin."

The *Shasta Courier* gave this harsh description of Redding:

They come with their families and furniture, the transportation of which takes all their spare cash, but living on the infatuation that Redding will soon make up for all; they rent a house and go into debt—and then the true state of affairs dawns on them. What are they to do? Poverty stares them in the face. The few things that they have are sold to stem the tide of starvation . . . .

Such utterances and the persistent frustration of too

Above: *This 1890s view down California Street looking southeast from Tehama Street, shows the Alta House and other businesses standing where the double-deck parking lot for the Downtown Redding Mall is now located. California Street was Redding's first main street, with most of the commercial activity facing westward toward the railroad tracks. Courtesy, Maida Glover Gandy*

Opposite page, top: *This circa 1910 photograph shows about half of the McCormick-Saeltzer grocery department. The store fronted the entire block on the west side of Market Street between Yuba and Placer streets and was divided into various departments. In terms of size and inventory, McCormick-Saeltzer was rated the biggest retail establishment between Sacramento and Portland for most of its lifespan. The store was destroyed by fire in January 1940. Courtesy, Shasta Historical Society*

Opposite page, bottom: *Charles Caminetti is shown here in the doorway of his "groceteria" at 1510 Market Street, circa 1930. In the days before supermarkets, small owner-operated stores featured compact inventories and incentives like home delivery, credit sales, and the latest in local gossip. Courtesy, Shasta Historical Society*

many teamsters vying for the hauling of two few goods probably accounted for the city's early nickname of "Poverty Flat."

But the city grew, only occasionally boss-ruled, and far from servile, eventually becoming the stable community it is today, hardly fulfilling the Shasta businessmen's dire prophecy.

A two-story building at the corner of Shasta and Market streets, built of native red clay, became the city hall in 1907. It served a community of 3,000 then, and housed the offices of city clerk, attorney, assessor, judge, town marshal, and justice of the peace. The board of trustees began regular meetings upstairs, a practice continued by city councils from 1937 to 1979, when the building was declared unsafe.

City police, tenants since 1912, moved into a remodeled automobile agency building on California Street a block away, and the agency's showroom was converted into the present city council chambers. Built at a cost of $10,000, the building today is listed in the National Register of Historic Places and is the target of a $429,000 rehabilitation project. A citizens committee is raising $80,000 toward the project, to augment city and federal funds. Restoration calls for a return to exterior and interior appearances of 1907 with a ninety-four-seat theater and an exhibition gallery. *Redding Report,* a quarterly publication of the city, in October 1985 called it "the only historical public building of significance left in Redding."

That description may be a bit unfair. Although it no

Above: *The Little Pine Street School, shown here circa 1915, was the first schoolhouse built in Redding. Constructed in 1873 on the east side of Pine Street between Placer and Yuba streets, the building stood until 1959 when it was removed for a municipal parking lot. Courtesy, Ray and Rika Coffelt*

Top: *Shown here circa 1900, the Castle Rock Springs Hotel, built by George Washington Bailey in 1895 near what is today Castle Crags State Park, served travelers for many years. A mineral spring was discovered near the hotel by miners in 1860, leading to the development of the Castle Rock Mineral Springs Company which bottled the zesty water. Courtesy, Shasta Historical Society*

longer belongs to the public, Redding's historic Pine Street School building is a thriving complex of professional offices and other businesses.

Some early businesses in Redding promoted themselves any way they could. Ads in *Purple and White*, the Shasta County High School publication of February 1901, tell of the Golden Eagle block of Yuba Street, which included a jewelry store, the Walker Brothers restaurant—"home of fancy mocha and java coffee"—and the shop of Charles Piftschek, the "merchant tailor."

In the nearby Bush block could be found P. Edgeberg's bicycle shop, no doubt with a bicycle built-for-two; Jacobson's Cash Store opposite the Temple Hotel offered dry goods, hats, and furnishings.

One of the most successful early businesses was Redding's "big store," the McCormick-Saeltzer Company. Anchoring the downtown area at Market and Yuba streets, it sold everything from women's corsets, kid gloves, silks, satins, "and other essentials of commodious living" to gunpowder. The store also became an agent for "celebrated Studebaker wagons," Oliver chilled plows, Grant Powder, and Connecticut Fire Insurance. The partners established branch stores in the mining communities of Keswick, Carrville, and De La Mar.

Meanwhile others were making a living from real estate. D.N. Honn, calling himself the "Land Man of Northern California," sold bottomland along the Sacra-

Above: *This circa 1925 photograph shows prunes drying on racks in the sun at the Nibarger Ranch in Shasta County. As agriculture became an important part of the regional economy, various crops were planted on a trial basis. Rice, olives, and strawberries were harvested in the Happy Valley and Municipal Airport areas. Courtesy, Shasta Historical Society*

Left: *Miss Jennie P. Bailey, shown here circa 1890, exemplifies the transition her hometown of Redding was undergoing—the frontier town was becoming more sophisticated and starting to put on airs. Miss Bailey, whose father operated Reid's Ferry, was called the prettiest girl in Shasta County. Courtesy, Shasta Historical Society*

mento River for thirty dollars an acre. John George owned the Pennsylvania House Hotel at the corner of California and Placer streets.

New businesses also included the Redding Reduction Works, with "assaying at Eastern Prices," and the Redding Foundry and Machine Works. By 1886 Redding was harboring the beginnings of a lumber industry. Cooper and Dean operated the Redding Planing Mill, while A.R. Chase and W.A. Peeples had the Bunker Hill Sawmill.

As agriculture made its appearance, I. Simon and Brothers' "The Grange" store was offering parasols, ladies' hats, "lawns and ginghams," ladies' gauze vests, men's summer suits, "linen and mohair dusters," and men's and boys' straw hats—not the sort of garb one might expect in a frontier town. But Redding already was putting on airs. It had an opera house early in its existence, and was beginning to adopt schooling and other forms of cultured civilization.

Redding also had the railroad and it wasn't long before the tracks provided an excursion run for curious Californians from Sacramento, San Francisco Bay, and other southland communities. Inns like Southern's, destined to become a way-stop for such important visitors as President Rutherford B. Hayes, were already developing in the primitive beauty of the Sacramento River Canyon north of the city.

Traveling shows like the Sells Brothers Circus, which came to town in 1886, marked the city as a ready stop for entertainment. Other famous expositions passed through town, including Buffalo Bill Cody's Wild West Show which was staged at what is now Tiger Field in the early 1900s. (Cody supposedly put up $10,000 to start the Anderson Water Company, operated originally by his two nephews who constructed a closed system of redwood flumes in the nearby town of Anderson.)

While Redding was enjoying this growth, Shasta, the "Queen City," put up quite a fight to remain the county's leading community.

In October 1886, scarcely six months before Redding's incorporation, a coalition that included Shasta businessmen James E. Isaacs, E. Lewin, John V. Scott, Henry Blumb, and A. Grotefend argued eloquently but futilely in a special supplement to the *Courier* against moving the courthouse from Shasta to Redding. This "executive committee" charged that Redding's "aggressors and agitators of 1882" (a group that, in that year,

had tried unsuccessfully to wrest the courthouse from Shasta's grasp) were up to their old tricks.

When the county was created by the legislature in 1850 with the Oregon border as its first northern boundary and Major Reading's ranchero as its first seat of government, the courthouse was soon moved from Reading's ranchero to Shasta. There it remained, first in a log building constructed in 1854, then in a brick building built in 1855 by James Loag and sold to the county in 1861 for $17,000.

The committee warned that if Shasta lost the courthouse, the U.S. land office would soon follow, and county residents would have even less need to visit the Queen City. The courthouse transfer, committee members said, would increase the county tax bill by $58,625 and almost certainly hike the $2.25 ad valorem tax rate. Gas and water would be added to county expenses as well as insurance costs, they warned.

The committee also questioned why it was necessary to move the courthouse to Redding when Shasta was only a twenty-cent trip away from the railroad depot, a cost more than offset, they said, by "Shasta's fine, bracing mountain air and it's pure and healthy water." Could one imagine, they asked, the health problems a juror would encounter trying to deliberate a verdict in Redding's summer heat?

Finally, the committee implored *Courier* readers, it was a matter of honor. Alleging that Redding was acting to gain supremacy in county affairs, a charge no doubt true, the panel noted that "old decried Shasta" was now being cast aside after having brought the telegraph to the county, paid $1,000 toward the railroad survey, and met Redding halfway with $6,400 on the cost of a new road between the two communities.

Of Redding, the Shasta businessmen said: "Her henchmen proclaim she is now the biggest town in the county and is to become the biggest in the whole north of the state by virtue of her wealth, her progress, her energy, her intellect and her liberality in county matters." But at too high a price, they lamented, "Shasta must be shorn of her dignity, broken down entirely and, if possible, her name and honor dragged low."

One might have heard violins at that point. But though eloquent, the paean was the last gasp of a dying community.

The courthouse was lost to Redding in 1888, a year after the city's incorporation and, as the committee predicted, the federal land office followed in 1890.

Above: *When Redding became the new county seat in 1888, an impressive new courthouse was built to house the heads of county government. This photograph, taken on the south steps of the courthouse in June 1890, shows the county's early leaders. In the back row from left to right are: James Issaks, district attorney; Albert F. Ross, clerk-auditor and recorder; Marshall Mitchell, town marshal of Redding; James Leary, deputy recorder under Ross; Judge Bell (white beard); Sheriff William Hopping; and George Fowler, deputy auditor. In the front row, seated left to right are: Tom Smith, deputy county clerk under Ross; Al Erwin, deputy sheriff; Trudy Welch, county superintendent of schools; Quint Adkins, county assessor; Andy Woodward; William Jackson, county treasurer; and George Albro, courthouse custodian. Courtesy, Shasta State Historic Park Courthouse Museum*

The original Shasta County Courthouse, circa 1915, appears on the right, with the bronzed Lady Justice high atop the copper-skinned dome. The more recent Hall of Records was added to its left. Courtesy, Shasta State Historic Park Courthouse Museum

A Time
of Promise

When Halley's Comet streaked across the nighttime sky in 1910, Shasta County residents were witnessing another star rising in their midst—the growing city of Redding.

It was a promising time for Redding. The early battles had been won. The county courthouse left Shasta and was relocated in Redding in 1888. Shasta County High School was started in 1898 to advance the educations of youngsters who learned their three R's in dozens of makeshift country schools. Rugby and cricket were played on the green fields of Keswick before the smelters came. The business panic of 1893 was receding and the mines were in full production again. While life for miners continued to be one of hard work for low pay, the mines' payrolls were planking the economic foundations of the community.

The county also shared the nation's sense of destiny. The western frontier had been conquered, the Civil War was a thing of the past, and the United States was becoming a unified nation.

Before 1914 the intermittent quarrels of other nations seemed remote and of little consequence. But events intruded from near and afar. The devastating earthquake that struck San Francisco in 1906 brought hundreds of scared refugees northward, some to stay. The Redding community, in turn, responded generously. The Mammoth Copper Company of Kennett and its miners sent $1,000 for relief, and Redding housewives baked all day to send a freight carload of bread to the stricken city. Other cars were loaded with cooking utensils and domestic goods, part of an outpouring

Though the streets were still unpaved, Redding added fancy electric streetlights in 1915. Placed on concrete bases in the center of each main intersection, the lights added a cosmopolitan feeling, especially after dark. This photograph shows market Street from the south. Glover's Garage and the McCormick-Saeltzer store are on the left. Courtesy, Maida Glover Gandy

from every community in the north state. By April 28, 1906, Shasta County's contributions totaled $17,500. In addition, Redding fed supper to a trainload of over 400 refugees on their way north one night.

San Francisco recovered in time for its grand Panama-Pacific Exposition of 1915. In Redding, that event was copied in what some have called the "Great Fair of 1915." It was literally a festival of lights, for it signaled the advent of electric streetlights in the city, made possible years earlier by Lord William Keswick and H.H. Noble, who installed the Volta powerhouse on Battle Creek to the southeast.

Lord Keswick joined economic forces with San Francisco financier Noble to bring electricity from Battle Creek southeast of Redding to Iron Mountain Mine.

They formed the Keswick Light and Power Company, which later became the Northern California Power Company until it was merged with Pacific Gas and Electric Company. The city bought power from Keswick and Noble until it began generating its own power from a plant by the river in 1921 in what is now Lake Redding Park. And so Redding has had its own power since 1921.

World War I took its toll on the community, with young men going off to fight and their elders organizing Liberty Bond rallies while wives and mothers held coffee klatches to roll bandages.

Among the returning soldiers were Judge Albert F. Ross and teacher Loren Ewing, who started a tradition of toasting the Armistice at 11:00 a.m. each November 11 in the old Golden Eagle Hotel. After the hotel burned in 1962, the toasts were continued in the Redding Elks Club. Though both men are now deceased, the toasts continue in their names, carried on by veterans of more recent wars.

Many early residents were demonstrating remarkable talent and bravado. One such resident was Dr. Thomas "Doc" Wyatt, founder of Memorial Hospital, the forerunner of Redding Medical Center. Wyatt lived such a cavalier existence that he became known in some circles as Redding's "Doc Holliday." When raging waters marooned four construction workers on the flood-swollen Sacramento River in the 1940 deluge, Wyatt steered his small motorboat twice into the torrent to rescue them from almost certain drowning. Salty and flamboyant, Wyatt died on November 29, 1973. One Redding resident described him as a "kindly, crusty

character who let his heart rule his head."

The Frisbie family produced a long line of civic developers. Edward Frisbie, who had the courage and foresight to purchase the remainder of B.B. Redding's 100 original lots in 1872, founded the Bank of Northern California, housed in a brick building on the southeast corner of Yuba and Market streets, in 1880. The Frisbie family then opened a second bank, the Redding Savings Bank, in 1911 for savings accounts and personal loans. This bank served as a depository for gold and silver which miners exchanged for goods at the nearby McCormick-Saeltzer store and other businesses.

Recalling the 1906 quake, Frisbie's grandson, Edward Charles Frisbie who also became a banker, said it "was the toughest time for Pacific Coast banks." As a young cashier he was sent to straighten out his bank's affairs in the stricken city. Frisbie found a nightmare of flaming confusion with the great banking houses in ruins. Yet he managed to do more than straighten out the bank's affairs; he was named bank president when his Uncle Nathan died in 1919, and later became manager in Redding for the Anglo California Bank, when the two banks were merged in 1934. Frisbie retired in 1949, leaving the bank known as Crocker Bank until its merger with Wells Fargo Bank in 1986.

Despite the Frisbies' and other leaders' efforts, banking was slow to develop in the county, and so too Redding's own growth. From 1920 until 1930 the population of the city and county remained virtually at a standstill.

However, frontier journalism thrived. At one time there were no less than four daily newspapers and a host of weeklies. Shasta, Millville, Anderson, and other communities all had early newspapers. The *Shasta Courier* was second only to the *Alta Californian* among the earliest Northern California papers. Even Horsetown had its *Northern Argus,* a literary gem that kept track of events in the now-extinct community.

But none could claim the power and influence that John P. Scripps Newspapers brought to town with the arrival of Paul C. Bodenhamer and Harry Bostwick in 1938. Their first—and for a long time, only—reporter was Dick Mallery, who covered major events leading to Shasta Dam's construction.

The *Redding Record,* established in 1938, became the *Record Searchlight and Courier-Free Press,* claiming a publishing lineage back to the *Shasta Courier* itself (which ceased production in the 1940s.) Bodenhamer guided the paper from a weekly to a daily that had a commanding circulation in three counties when he retired in 1972 as editor emeritus. The reins were turned over to Robert W. Edkin, previously of the Ventura *Star-Free Press,* who took the newspaper editorially in a more conservative direction.

In the early years of Redding's newspapers, the writing was rugged, ragged, and sometimes rudely arrogant. But few reached the inflammatory degree of General Samuel Dosh, the *Shasta Courier* editor who lashed out at political opponents and minorities alike with often intemperate remarks.

In later years, a colorful publisher who also practiced medicine was Earnest "Doc" Dozier, publisher of the weekly *Shasta Dial.* Charles J. "Chick" Gleeson also lent his writing talents to the community, coming to Redding from Billings, Montana. Gleeson worked his way up to become the *Record Searchlight's* managing editor, leaving the paper for newspapers in Willows and Colusa. After his retirement he became a local historian, publishing several books.

Due to Gleeson, Veronica Satorius, and others, Redding has a well-defined history of its churches. Gleeson and Satorius report the first missionary at Shasta was a man named Father Francis Martin Schwenninger. Better known as Father Florian, Schwenninger served in Shasta from 1853 to 1855 and was followed by Father Raphael Rainaldi, whose dream to build a church didn't get beyond the foundation that today is part of the Shasta Historical Monument.

Methodists and Catholics were among the earliest church fonders in Shasta County, the Methodists spreading the gospel through circuit-riding preachers while Catholic priests set up parishes in Shasta, French Gulch, and Horsetown.

For Methodists, the fiery Reverend John B. Hill, a two-fisted evangelist, awakened spent celebrants on Sunday mornings by belting hymns from the Empire Hotel balcony in old Shasta. Hill arrived in Shasta on April 15, 1852, and preached from hotel balconies until he founded Shasta's Methodist Episcopal Church. He reportedly once threw a gambler off a hotel balcony for trying to stop his preaching. Hill also preached in Weaver (now Weaverville), approximately forty-five miles away from Shasta, and walked there once a week to save the eight-dollar cost of mule transportation.

One month later after Hill arrived, a lot was deeded for a Shasta church by William Bonafield, but it was left in favor of another. A church was built at a cost of $1,314.75.

When it burned down in 1858, the church was replaced by a Union Church building, which served a succession of Methodist preachers, including at one time John Wesley Harrow, the church trustee. Among parishioners were J.N. Chappell, who became a state assemblyman and Judge C.C. Bush, later Redding's first mayor; and F.C. Tiffin, county clerk.

Camp meetings and circuit riding spread the gospel to other congregations in the mining towns and camps. They were infrequently held in groves of trees near water for baptismal purposes. Usually they were joyous occasions for hymn singing, soul cleansing, and redemption. For some it was the only time of worship for as much as a year.

At one time a few Methodist preachers covered an astonishing forty-six locations in Shasta County. In 1878 the Reverend C.H. Darling not only preached in Redding and Anderson, but at fifteen other stops as well, covering them all in a two-week period. One such meeting place was used so often it became known as Piety Hill and was deeded to the church for construction of a meeting hall and parsonage in 1862 near the present community of Igo.

Another meeting place, a mining camp called Texas Springs, disappeared when the gold ran out. The home of poet Joaquin Miller, located one mile north of the settlement, was used for prayer meetings.

Other churches followed. B.B. Redding supplied the First Presbyterian Church—established in 1878 in his namesake community—with 245-pound bell, which was destroyed when the church burned on September 13,

Above: *This Baptist church was built in 1889 on the northeast corner of Court and Placer streets. The building was destroyed by a wind-swept fire that also destroyed the Baptist parsonage, St. Joseph Catholic Church, Redding Ice Factory, fifteen residences, and other private property. Courtesy, Veronica Satorius*

Left: *The Reverend John B. Hill founded the Methodist Episcopal Church in Shasta in the 1850s. Before he had a pulpit to preach from, Hill would often conduct services from a hotel balcony, awakening those trying to sleep off a hard-drinking Saturday night. Courtesy, Shasta Historical Society*

Above: *This circa 1925 photograph is a view of Market Street look-*
ing south. On the left is the old city hall and the Temple Hotel. On
the right is an early office for PG&E. Courtesy, Veronica Satorius

Opposite page: *The All Saints Episcopal Church was built on the*
southwest corner of Court and Yuba streets in 1902. The wooden-
frame building with the shingle exterior was appreciated by a congre-
gation that had been meeting in various rooms around town for the
previous ten years. Courtesy, Ray and Rika Coffelt

1915. The church was rebuilt by 1916. Meanwhile services were held in the Pine Street schoolhouse, where
Judge C.C. Bush's wife Ida led the choir. Among the early
members of the First Presbyterian Church was the
Edward Frisbie family.

The Baptists arrived with the First Baptist Church
in 1889, followed by such denominations as the Mormons, Seventh-day Adventists, Congregationalists, Lutherans, Unitarians, Christian Scientists, and Jehovah's
Witnesses. Other churches built in Redding before 1900
included the First Presbyterian (1881), Methodist
(1883), and Catholic (1885).

Among ethnic minorities, Chinese communities practiced Buddhism and Taoism. Ancestors of the late
Moon Lee—a state highway commissioner for several
years in the 1960s and a prominent Weaverville resident until his death in 1985—brought a Taoist temple
to the goldfields by ship and muleback in the 1850s.

In the late 1800s, some Indian sects practiced the
federally forbidden "ghost dancing" rituals in the Yolla
Bolla Mountains southwest of Redding. Indians also
attributed mystic powers to spirits dwelling in Mt.
Shasta.

Black immigrants founded the African Methodist

Episcopal Zion and Christian Methodist Episcopal churches in 1894. The Second Baptist Church and Willing Workers Church of God were later additions to the black religious community.

Religion has never lost its stronghold in the region. A splurge of church building took place in Redding in the 1960s and 1970s. When fire destroyed St. Joseph's Catholic Church in 1964, the church and parish school were rebuilt near Benton Airpark in west Redding. A second Catholic church was built in recent years in Shasta Meadows. Famed architect Frank Lloyd Wright designed the Pilgrim Congregational Church near the city's western boundary, pointing the church's center beam toward Mt. Shasta.

The Church of Jesus Christ of the Latter-day Saints built a church in then unincorporated Enterprise in 1965 at a cost of $412,000. The church serves as headquarters for nine wards in Shasta, Tehama, Trinity, and Siskiyou counties.

In east Redding the North Valley Baptist Church and other Baptist sects thrived, North Valley appealing to the young through its pastor, the Reverend Royal Blue.

More recent arrivals are the Neighborhood churches of Redding and Anderson, and the Little Country

Church, which recently began a program of Christmas and Easter pageants that seems destined to become a seasonal attraction.

But while the upright were doing good works, the lawless were committing their crimes.

Law enforcement in the 1850s and 1860s in Shasta County, as elsewhere in California, was rudimentary, often cruel, and sometimes unjust. Early communities formed vigilante committees, posses, and/or home militias—the terms varied.

What passed for justice was more often vengeance. Clashes with Indians led to retaliation far out of proportion to the crimes involved. If a settler was killed, dozens of tribesmen and even women and children were sometimes massacred in reprisal.

Editor W.O. Carter of the *Shasta Courier* blatantly demanded justice for the death of a young army officer by calling for the death of numerous Indians. His statements were condemned in the Bay area newpapers as racist and inflammatory.

Frontier justice often led to the noose. The courthouse at Shasta had a gibbet conveniently located in back of it.

One such hanging involved a robber named Baker and his accomplice who were convicted of killing a mailman and robbing him of receipts meant for the tax collector. Both Baker and another convicted murderer named Crouch were hanged in August 1878 in Shasta. Baker's "swan song" was a number of verses of "Wild, Wild Rose on the Mountain," while Crouch died silently.

The most celebrated case of lawlessness in early county history involved a stagecoach robbery in which Buck Montgomery, an express messenger and guard, was fatally shot as stage driver John Boyce was nearing the end of his journey to Redding from Weaverville on May 14, 1892. Montgomery was guarding two express boxes loaded with gold bullion. The stagecoach had a single passenger, a Mr. Suhr. In the exchange of gunfire, both Boyce and Suhr were shot in the legs. Montgomery felled one highwayman with a shot. As the horse team lunged in terror, Montgomery leaned out of the coach to fire two more shots before he was hit and collapsed.

Dr. B.E. Stevenson and his wife, out for a buggy ride, met the careening coach. The doctor stopped the horses and gave medical aid to the victims while Mrs. Stevenson went for help. Sheriff Thomas Greene and Deputy Chris Bidwell formed a posse. They found Charlie Ruggles the next day at the bottom of a canyon, near death from a wound in the mouth. John Ruggles, the other suspect, was arrested near Woodland after being wounded in a skirmish with officers.

Anger spread throughout the community, with demands calling for immediate judgment. On July 23, a Saturday night, young jailer George Albro was roused from sleep by a "masked mob of seventy-five men" (his accounting, no doubt, has been embellished over time).

The mob demanded Albro's keys to the jail. When Albro told them the keys were locked in a safe, he was blindfolded and placed in a corner. Two charges of black powder and sledgehammers were used to open the safe.

Cell doors were opened until the Ruggleses were found. Although John Ruggles insisted he alone was to blame for the robbery, both men were dragged to a tree near the railroad tracks and hanged. John was thirty-two years old and Charlie, twenty-six.

One robber who did get away with several stagecoach heists in Shasta County was Charles Bolton, alias "Black Bart," a genteel bandit who worked wearing a mask and duster, and carrying a shotgun.

James L. Richardson was active in Shasta County law enforcement for many years. Serving as under-sheriff to Charles H. Behrens from 1899 to 1901, Richardson was elected sheriff in 1902. The campaign card (inset) handed out by Richardson while seeking election in 1902 was about the size of a business card and was a popular form of vote-seeking at that time. Courtesy, Lake Shasta Caverns

Left: *Charles Bolton, alias "Black Bart," was a former schoolteacher turned stagecoach robber who pulled several heists in Shasta County. He was notorious for his snippets of poetry, and once declared, "If for any crime I'm hung, let it be for my verse." Courtesy, California State Library*

Below: *This 1901 photograph shows the interior of the sheriff's office of the Shasta County Courthouse. The man standing on the left is Sheriff Charles H. Behrens. James L. Richardson is seated in the back. Courtesy, Shasta Historical Society*

Above: Standing in front of the city hall looking over recovered booty are: (left to right) Earl Sholes, Scott Lincecum, and John Balma. Lincecum joined the police department in August of 1938 and served as chief of police from 1952 until 1966. Balma's illustrious law enforcement career began with the police department in 1939. Courtesy, Lon and Cindy McCasland

Opposite page: L.D. "Lou" Poole, right, Redding's first paid fire chief, and Will "Pop" Smith, the chief of police, are shown here circa 1915 in the fire chief's office in City Hall at Market and Shasta streets. Law enforcement and city administration blossomed with the needs of a growing population. Courtesy, Shasta Historical Society

A former schoolteacher, Black Bart usually left behind pieces of doggerel, once declaring, "If for any crime I'm hung, let it be for my verse." He was finally undone by a doggedly persistent Wells Fargo detective who traced him through a laundry tag in San Francisco.

Other notable bandits of those days included Rattlesnake Dick and Sheetiron Jack. The latter, it was said, outfitted himself with a pair of cast-iron sandwich boards. Sheetiron Jack was captured in trauma after a deputy scored a direct hit on his armor with a shotgun blast. Rattlesnake Dick supposedly left a $50,000 haul cached somewhere between Redding and Castle Crags which has never been found—a tribute perhaps to the veracity of the tale.

Sylvester Hull, the county's first sheriff, was followed by a line of sheriffs that ended in 1946 when the county sheriff's office was taken over by Redding's then-police chief John Balma. Redding and Shasta County achieved a rare stability in law enforcement in later years largely through the efforts of Sheriff Balma and Robert Whitmer, a career policeman who came to Redding from Illinois.

Whitmer succeeded retiring George Vanderpool as police chief on September 15, 1969, after a career that

included positions with the International Association of Police Chiefs and the Illinois Law Enforcement Commission. He arrived in Redding at a time when civil turmoil was rampant in the nation, although Redding escaped the disorders of other, larger communities. Under Whitmer, the police department was reorganized into the smooth-running agency it is today. Police methods and record systems were modernized, relations with the news media improved, and policemen held accountable for their actions.

A onetime Redding police chief, Balma was born in Kennett and spent thirty-six years in city and county law enforcement before his retirement in 1982. Called by some "the last of the Old West sheriffs," Balma shepherded the Sheriff's Department from a rural, antiquated law enforcement agency into a modern department respected throughout the nation.

The city and county departments took innovative steps such as the Student Training Orientation Program (STOP), which put policemen in classrooms as friendly advisers to children. Patterned after a similar, smaller program in the city of Davis, the program was lost in the budget cuts caused by Proposition 13, but it has survived in principle in youth-oriented programs sponsored by both the city and county departments.

During the 1970s and 1980s, Redding and Shasta County also made strides in treatment of jail and prison inmates. The county took over state-run Crystal Creek Conservation Camp west of Whiskeytown Lake in July 1972. Since then it has become a north state rehabilitation center for minimum security prisoners from Shasta and nine other counties.

A hunger strike by women prisoners protesting jail conditions in 1974 was a catalyst in seeking a new county jail and justice center. The state Department of Corrections investigated and found numerous violations in Shasta's Depression-era jail.

The state's report sparked a quest for state and federal funds. Eventually, the project grew into a nine-story, $17-million edifice that in 1986 was still the tallest building in Redding. Because of operational costs, it has developed into a regional facility.

A *Record Searchlight* probe in 1969 led to reforms and reorganization of the county's Juvenile Hall. The agency now has an enlarged, more professional staff. Law enforcement was further enhanced by a nine-county criminology service laboratory, established at Shasta College in September 1972. It was the first in the state, followed by others in Fresno, Santa Barbara, and Riverside.

Water Empowers
the County

S hasta County civic leaders recognized early in its history that the region had great potential for harnessing hydroelectric power.

The first efforts to develop it were made by small independent power companies. In the early 1900s the Northern California Power Company, a forerunner of Pacific Gas and Electric Company (PG&E), built a series of power installations on creeks in the eastern part of the county. Such powerhouses as Kilarc near Whitmore, about thirty miles east of Redding, churned tumbling creek waters into lighting for homes and industry locally and elsewhere. These installations, however, were mere toys compared to what was to come.

As Redding grew, flood control became a necessity upstream on the Sacramento River where it was joined by the Pit and McCloud rivers. Torrential winter rains caused tremendous flooding that drowned livestock, ruined croplands, and routed families to higher ground.

There was first a plan to build a dam in Iron Canyon, the whitewater section of river between Redding and Red Bluff. That plan fell through when opposition developed among farmers, ranchers, and orchardists in the Anderson and Cottonwood areas.

The Iron Canyon project would have inundated lowlands around both communities, backing up water to the present outskirts of Redding, which then would have had lakeside recreation on the city's southern flank. That plan was all but abandoned after Roscoe Anderson and other outspoken Redding civic leaders began campaigning for a dam that would catch the

On July 8, 1940, the first bucket of concrete was poured for the construction of Shasta Dam. The last bucket of concrete was poured on December 22, 1944. The total amount of concrete used in the construction of Shasta Dam and appurtenant works was 6,535,000 cubic yards. Courtesy, Shasta Historical Society

Above, right: *Roscoe Anderson, left, played a major role in attaining government approval for Shasta Dam construction. Anderson is shown here shaking hands with George Albro on Albro's eighty-fifth birthday. Albro was a custodian of the Shasta County courthouse for seventy-five years. Courtesy, Shasta Historical Society*

Right: *In 1902 a new transformer slowly made its way toward the powerhouse at Volta about thirty miles east of Redding. The heavy equipment was chained to a wagon with solid wooden wheels and pulled by nearly a dozen teams of horses. Courtesy, Pacific Gas & Electric Company*

Below: *This 1904 photograph shows the first dynamo for Kilarc Power House moving to its destination on a freight wagon with solid wooden wheels pulled by teams of horses. The power house was constructed on Old Cow Creek near Whitmore. For the most part development of electricity was ahead of the development of transportation which resulted in much agony in getting the generating components into the rugged generating sites in the mountains. Courtesy, Carl and Mollie St. John*

Opposite page: *Francis Christopher Carr, right, shown in his office with his secretary Jennie Woods, was born in Millville in 1875. From deputy district attorney, in 1906 he became a justice of the peace. Courtesy, Shasta Historical Society*

three troublemaking rivers where they joined in a deep canyon just north of Redding.

Anderson arrived in Redding in 1914 to become secretary-manager of the Shasta County Promotion and Development Association, an organization he described as "a committee, a name and a few hundred dollars." Before the year 1915 had ended, the resourceful Anderson had expanded this association to include four adjacent counties and changed its name to the Northern California Counties Association.

The fight for Shasta Dam was just beginning when Anderson arrived. He was appointed to the newly-created State Water Commission by Governor Hiram Johnson, an appointment that led to a lasting friendship with the governor, who later became a U.S. senator.

In the 1920s Anderson served as a Republican assemblyman for six years. He moved into the heat of the water fight as chairman of a subcommittee that held hearings on the proposed dam.

Anderson said in a 1971 interview, at age ninety-one, that Shasta Dam was proposed to block a movement for the Iron Canyon dam that would flood prime agricultural and industrial land. "We decided instead of fighting we'd promote a larger idea and we did," he said.

Raised in an impoverished midwestern farm family, Anderson was used to challenges. He was nine years old when his father was ruined by a drought, fourteen when he began farming for himself, a teacher in early adulthood, and a stereopticon technician after the San Francisco earthquake of 1906. Anderson enrolled that year in Stanford University and later earned a law degree at the University of Nebraska. While in Lincoln, Nebraska, he met William Jennings Bryan and became friends with the famous orator. Anderson's own political career included a losing race to become state senator and a brief flirtation with the idea of running for lieutenant governor.

Anderson did, however, win election as Redding's mayor during World War II. He also found time to dabble in real estate, edit a weekly newspaper, and take part in the first survey team to lay out a highway north of Redding in the Sacramento River Canyon.

Anderson's efforts in the Shasta Dam debate were taken up by Judge Francis P. Carr. A former justice of the peace, Carr became recognized as an attorney on water matters when he helped to form the Anderson-Cottonwood Irrigation District in 1914 to 1916.

Carr had fought the Iron Canyon Dam project for forty years, and became interested in Shasta Dam while serving as a state water commissioner appointed by Governor James Rolph.

Born in Millville, the son of a pioneer teacher, Carr later served as Shasta County deputy district attorney under Thomas B. Dozier, and formed the Redding law firm of Carr and Kennedy with Laurence Kennedy, Sr. When Carr died on August 21, 1944, editor Paul Bodenhamer of the *Record Searchlight* called him "one of the big men of his generation." His memory is preserved in the Judge Francis Carr Powerhouse at Whiskeytown Lake.

Another who joined in the Shasta Dam fight was John McColl, a Redding dairyman who later became a state senator. Co-founder with John Fitzpatrick, Sr., of McColls Dairy, McColl died in an automobile accident in 1938.

Proponents of Shasta Dam determined early on that the proposed dam size was beyond the capacities of state financing and clearly a job for the federal government. Carr and McColl journeyed to Washington, D.C., to lobby for funds for the dam project during the 1930s. Carr's son Laurence, a Redding attorney, recalls the pair were often so short of traveling money that they stayed in his Georgetown University apartment which he shared with three roommates.

The commission helped Shasta County community leaders work Shasta Dam into the slowly developing State Water Plan with the dam as the keystone of the plan's Central Valley Project (CVP).

Opposition developed from Pacific Gas and Electric Company and other interests. PG&E had much at stake with its system of smaller dam projects and its interlocking power sources. Carr, who organized a statewide promotional effort for Shasta Dam, at one time offered to turn in his portfolio as a PG&E attorney—an offer that was never accepted.

At one point the giant project, which cost $120 million (which would return that amount multifold over the years), depended upon a pass-the-hat campaign to keep voters from defeating it altogether in a statewide referendum. The dam proposal was approved as a keystone of the giant Central Valley Project, a plan to satisfy the state's water and power needs for the next half-century.

Shasta Dam required six years to build. Its dimensions are awesome. Completed in September 1944, the dam is taller than the Washington Monument. Its spillway is three times the height of Niagara Falls. It is second in mass only to Grand Coulee Dam in Washington State, and, at 517 feet, second in height only to Hoover Dam in Arizona.

More than 6.5 million feet of concrete and 13,000 tons of reinforced steel went into the massive structure. A construction contract was awarded July 6, 1938, to Pacific Constructors, Inc., a consortium of twelve firms which eventually employed some 4,000 workers. The project resembled a movie set as conceived by

Left: *This 1942 view of Shasta Dam during construction shows the lake bed already cleared behind the dam and the shoreline established. The dam was put together in a series of blocks or cubes, each poured full of concrete separate from the others. The color of the dam lightened as the concrete cured. Courtesy, Bureau of Reclamation, Shasta Dam*

Below: *Hard work was the bottom line in the construction of Shasta Dam. The men pictured here were called "high scalers"; held in place by safety ropes around their waists, they operated high-speed rock drills on the sheer face of cliffs that were to become the resting place for the concrete bulk of Shasta Dam. Courtesy, Bureau of Reclamation, Shasta Dam*

Opposite page: *This 1948 photograph shows Shasta Dam construction workers applying finishing touches to the spillway apron at the base of the dam. A portion of the power house can be seen at the right; in the distance stands a bridge across the Sacramento River still in service today. Excavation of the riverbed below the spillway area was still taking place at this time. Courtesy, Bureau of Reclamation, Shasta Dam*

Right: *Today little remains of what was once the longest conveyor belt in the world, shown here in 1940. During Shasta Dam's construction, the yard-wide belt moved at a rate of about six miles per hour over a nine and one-half mile course. There were twenty-six separate sections to the belt, each powered by a 200-horsepower engine. Courtesy, Bureau of Reclamation, Shasta Dam*

Below: *This view looks south from the north end of the Southern Pacific Railroad trestle, built about 1940 to reroute the tracks out of the Sacramento River canyon due to the construction of Shasta Dam. The impressive trestle channeled rail traffic in a northerly course and at an elevation that would not be inundated by the waters of the new Shasta Lake. Courtesy, Vivian Harrigan*

Opposite page: *Looking north up Market Street from Butte Street, this circa 1945 scene shows a bustling downtown. Shasta Dam was under construction and generated much activity. The palm trees stand in front of what is now the Old City Hall at Market and Shasta streets. The portion of Market Street in the foreground is now part of the Downtown Redding Mall. Courtesy, Vivian Harrigan*

Cecil B. DeMille as workers toiled like ants to pour buckets of liquid concrete swung on lines radiating from a giant central steel tower. The tower was eventually cut off several hundred feet below the lake's full surface so it wouldn't harm boats. The base of it can still be seen during drought years when the lake level is low.

Contractor Henry Kaiser dared to build a belt-line conveyor 9.6 miles long from Redding's present civic auditorium area to carry gravel to the construction site for mixing with water and powdered cement. Kaiser's brainchild helped to launch his shipbuilding and real estate empire.

Building the dam required diversion of the Sacramento River through an old railroad tunnel while the railroad itself was rerouted to Redding at a cost of fourteen million dollars, which was added to that of the dam, power plant, and related projects.

Construction stiffs tell harrowing stories of the job hazards. Glenn Jeffries, who worked from 1938 to 1942 as a drill operator, recalled that many were killed and

others left maimed by accidents on the huge project. A flood in February 1940 ripped out a coffer dam and otherwise wreaked havoc on the dam project, damaging a new Highway 99 bridge (now the city's North Market Street bridge).

The contribution of Shasta Dam to Redding's—and the state's—future cannot be overemphasized. For Redding, the dam accelerated growth, brought unprecedented prosperity, and changed the landscape north of the city for all time.

Since an enormous flood threat in 1979, there have been studies about raising the dam another 200 feet at an estimated cost of $1.4 billion (1978 prices) to increase water storage capacity to fourteen million acre feet.

Before the dam was built, mining fumes had virtually denuded the area's forests around the dam site of vegetation, causing heavy winter runoffs that made lowland areas around Redding virtually untenable. James K. Carr, a son of Judge Carr who later served as undersecretary of the Department of Interior under

Above: *Clair A. Hill held the position of Deputy County Engineer in Redding from 1938 to 1941. In 1945, he opened a small engineering business which through the years blossomed into an institution of international scope. Courtesy, Clair and Joan Hill*

Opposite page, top: *These Trinity River Project workers are tying steel reinforcing rods, which look like the rib cage of a giant whale, to form a concrete tunnel for water conduction. Courtesy, Redding Museum and Art Center*

Opposite page, bottom: *Building a huge earthen dam on the Trinity River and piping the water through a range of rugged mountains to a hydroelectric generating facility was a big job by any standard. This arc welder is working on penstocks in 1960. Courtesy, Redding Museum and Art Center*

President John F. Kennedy, undertook restoration of the ridges while he was serving as an engineer for the reclamation bureau out of Chico. One method used after World War II was to reclaim mats made of steel for improvised military airfields and install them on the eroded hillsides as erosion soil catchers.

Through the city now could buy its own power from the federal government, after the completion of Shasta Dam the state still needed more irrigation water and even more energy. And so there have been other large projects in Shasta County and neighboring Trinity County—before nuclear and petroleum power, hydroelectric power was king. Dams and powerhouses were built feverishly in an effort to harness the water and power needed for California's growing population. To that end the Trinity River Project (TRP) was established in the late 1950s and early 1960s.

Unlike Shasta, TRP relied on a complex of dams and diversion tunnels to bring water stored on the westbound Trinity River into the southbound Sacramento River for delivery to Southern California customers via the Central Valley Project.

Much of the planning for TRP orginated in the Redding engineering office of Clair A. Hill and Associates, destined to become a linchpin of the international engineering firm of CH2M-Hill. Born in Redding, where he swam in the Sacramento River in his boyhood and roamed the wilderness, Hill opened his engineering office during the Depression in a wood-frame house opposite the courthouse. An oddity of architecture, the house is still inside the CH2M-Hill building, captured forever within outer walls of brick and mortar.

The river project was among the last great hydroelectric projects comleted before widespread reaction of conservationists to damming more streams cooled the dam building fervor in the 1970s.

Like Shasta Dam, the building of Trinity Dam and related projects sparked a construction boom in Redding that carried the city's economy through much of the 1960s. The city served as a railroad and highway terminal for equipment and materials. And also like Shasta Dam, which fostered hastily built shantytowns in the Central Valley area north of Redding, TRP brought its swarms of workers to create populations overnight near construction sites.

Unlike Shasta, however, Trinity Dam was earthfill. The Trinity Dam Contractors, a combine headed by Guy F. Atkinson Company, won the contract on a bid

Whiskeytown Lake is nestled in the foothills approximately nine miles west of Redding. Constructed as part of the extensive Trinity River Project, the lake also serves as a pleasant camping and recreation site. Highway 299W is shown winding its way around the lake's northern perimeter. Photo by Tom Dunlap. Courtesy, Record Searchlight

of more than forty-nine million dollars to build the dam north of Weaverville.

During the six-year project, "hundreds of men bored tunnels, tamped concrete and steel for powerhouses, and hauled thousands of tons of earth and rock," the *Record Searchlight* reported in 1964. An estimated 750 men worked on the Trinity project during peak construction in the spring of 1963. The total project cost was $253 million.

Like other large construction projects, TRP was plagued with labor problems. Work stopped when equipment operators walked off the job in February 1961. A widespread strike of construction laborers again shut down the project in May 1962, idling some 10,000 workmen in the north state; a wildcat strike of tunnel workers briefly tied up operations in 1963. In each case the dispute was over wages and benefits keyed to an inflationary economy. None of the strikes stopped the project for long, however.

A construction feature of Trinity Dam was the beltline conveyor, two miles long, that brought rock from Pettijohn Mountain down nine flights (belt sections) to be mixed with borrowed earth for tamping into the dam base.

The grand strategy of TRP was awesome in its simplicity. Briefly, the project was to trap and store

Trinity River water in a small dam near Lewiston in Trinity County and divert it through a tunnel under Hoadley Peak to the valley occupied by historic Whiskeytown. The plan meant the razing of Whiskeytown and the relocation of its pioneer cemetery to a point downstream of newly constructed Whiskeytown Dam.

Whiskeytown Dam, which dams Clear Creek a few miles west of Redding, creates a constant-level holding basin where the Trinity River water is siphoned as needed underground to the Sacramento River upstream from Keswick Dam. Clear Creek tunnel workers "holed through" the eleven-mile, $36-million tunnel at 4:30 a.m. on July 28, 1960. Mike Roch and Dan Daggs, superintendents of crews working from opposite directions, sealed the occasion with a handshake.

The Clear Creek powerhouse at the west side of Whiskeytown Lake was then started in June 1963,

The Trinity River Dam Project of 1961 required tunnels to be carved out of rock for water to travel from the dam near Lewiston through the mountains to the Judge Francis Carr Power House at Whiskeytown Lake, and then through more mountains to the Spring Creek Power House near Keswick Lake. Courtesy, Redding Museum and Art Center

along with an extra transmission line to link TRP power with the Central Valley Project.

Trinity water flowed through the tunnel for the first time March 25, 1963, when Phil Walters, a U.S. government engineer, pressed a button at the intake tower at Lewiston Lake, and water dropped through penstocks to churn the powerhouse generators.

Trinity Dam was finished in 1961. Stewart L. Udall, secretary of the Department of Interior for President John F. Kennedy, spoke at the dedication of Trinity Dam on October 14, 1961. Kennedy himself dedicated Whiskeytown Dam two years later, just weeks before his assassination.

The Whiskeytown Dam project, begun in August 1960 by Gibbons and Reed Construction Company on a $6.2-million contract, created a lake with thirty-six miles of shoreline which changed Redding's recreation scene in many ways. One event is the annual Whiskeytown Regatta, which draws hundreds of sailing craft during Memorial Day weekend. Redding voters made the lake a keystone of the Shasta-Trinity-Whiskeytown National Recreation Area in 1962 during a special election.

One might think that two giant hydroelectric projects would be enough for one county, but another project was soon underway once again.

PG&E applied on May 8, 1962, to the state Public Utilities Commission for permission to begin a $92-million project to harness more power on the Pit and McCloud rivers above the Shasta Lake level. At that time the largest hydroelectric project in PG&E history, the McCloud-Pit project cost more than $100 million before its completion in 1965. The project added 330 kilowatts of generation to the PG&E system and included four reservoirs, two tunnels, three powerhouses, and three transmission lines of varying lengths (the longest was a fourteen-mile stretch to a substation at Round Mountain).

McCloud-Pit involved eighteen contractors and approximately 1,000 workmen. A special camp was constructed to house many of the workers during the three-year project.

Dedication rites were performed June 3, 1966, at the McCloud powerhouse area. The powerhouse was dedicated to the memory of James B. Black, a former PG&E president. Black's two sons, Charles and John, were present. An honored guest was Charles Black's wife, the former child movie star and soon-to-be diplo-

mat, Shirley Temple Black.

Dam building at last ceased after this project, although there were several aborted efforts to interest the government in building dams on Cow and Stillwater creeks east of Redding. A proposed two-dam project to harness water and power on forks of Cottonwood Creek on the Shasta-Tehama boundary has been proposed and discussed since the 1960s without getting beyond the study stage.

For alternative energy resources, Redding joined the eleven-city Northern California Power Association in the 1970s. The city's voters, however, rejected a chance to buy into the $4.3 billion Palo Verde nuclear plant about fifty miles west of Phoenix, Arizona, in April 1982, forcing the city to give up its twenty-five-megawatt allotment to the 66,000-customer Modesto Irrigation District. As the year 1985 ended, Redding was still sorting out alternatives for more power, including a proposal to harness runoff from Spring Creek on Iron Mountain for additional hydroelectricity. In 1986, Redding dedicated a hydroelectric power plant for the city at Whiskeytown Dam.

Above and opposite page: *On September 28, 1963, President John Fitzgerald Kennedy delivered his dedication speech at Whiskeytown Dam before an estimated crowd of 10,000. Only weeks later he was assassinated. Courtesy, Clair and Joan Hill (above); Veronica Satorius (opposite page)*

Forests Bring
Big Business

When Samuel Hensley chopped down trees and floated logs down the Sacramento River to Sutter's Fort in the late 1840s, he became the first logger of record in Shasta County.

He was not, however, the first to fell trees in the area. Before Hensley's arrival, trappers hewed lodgepole pine into winter lean-tos and sheepherders and other early settlers built crude cabins against the weather. But Hensley was the first in the county to log for profit, and was a pioneer in the area's primary industry.

The early lumber trade was rudimentary in nature. At first lumber was produced entirely for local consumption. A factor in retarding the industry was the sheer amount of effort required to cut down trees and turn them into boards. The "misery whip," a long, crosscut saw, played a role in tree-cutting, living up to its name. (Cumbersome dragsaws, the forerunner of chainsaws, replaced the misery whips in the 1930s.)

Transporting logs and boards was awkward, too, because of their great weight and bulk. Oxen were used to span the distance between stump and sawmill until the animals were replaced by steam-driven tractors.

Early sawmills usually consisted of a pit over which a log was positioned. One man stood in the pit and another at ground level and together they cut the log using the misery whip.

The trick was to pull the saw through the cut with a minimum of whip on the trailing end. Two men working in rhythm could cut an astonishing amount of lumber in a day, but the work was slow and physically

Logging railroads were common in the woods surrounding Redding. Localities such as Weed, LaMoine, McCloud, Pondosa, Round Mountain, Bella Vista, and much of eastern Shasta County were served by logging railroads. The train in this photograph, taken about 1905, was owned by the Terry Lumber Company of Round Mountain. Courtesy, Tom and Frances Dunlap

Above: *Loggers pictured here prepare to hook a team of yoked oxen to a wagon prior to hauling the logs to the sawmill. Beasts of burden such as horses and oxen were first used to move cut timber from the woods to the mill. It was a slow and dangerous method that eventually gave way to steam-powered tractors and locomotives. Courtesy, Charlotte Engle*

Opposite page: *One reason local timber became such big business was because the timber was so big. Jeff Reed (right) and a Mr. Benton, father of Hart Benton who built an early sawmill near Shingletown, stand with their crosscut saw, or "misery whip," as their faithful dog oversees the operation. Courtesy, Shasta Historical Society*

punishing. Some primitive sawmills, particularly in the Whitmore and Shingletown areas, speeded up the process by using waterwheels to power rachets that moved the saws.

Trees were plentiful, laborers abundant, and lumber cheap, so early buildings were thrown together without thought of permanence. Devastating fires were frequent and usually all-consuming. The only recourse was to rebuild as quickly as possible.

Shasta boasted the county's first sawmill, a two-man small whipsaw pit mill which cut boards for residential and commercial buildings. But the lumber industry grew to benefit Shasta's more vigorous neighbor. Situated downhill from a second "golden crescent" of commercial timber, Redding naturally evolved into a lumber trade center and an industrial focal point of the wood products industry.

By 1886 Redding already had the makings of a lumber town. The Redding Planing Mill was operated by Cooper and Dean, while A.R. Chase and W.A. Peeples had the Bunker Hill Sawmill, an offshoot of the Bun-

Above: *Whitmore in the early 1900s was a home for loggers, a resting spot for travelers, and a center for mail dispersal. In 1903, when this photograph was taken, the Whitmore Hotel, Post Office, and feed barn all claimed L.O. Sheridan as the proprietor. From left to right are Mrs. L.O. Sheridan, Mrs. Owen Dailey, Margaret Sheridan, Grandma Sheridan, Miss Dunham, and Mrs. Joe Dunham. The two boys in the wooden wagon are George Sheridan and his cousin. Courtesy, Carl and Mollie St. John*

Opposite page: *This photo, taken in 1900 by the legendary photographer B.F. Loomis, shows members of the Thatcher family plus some of the working crew gathered on and around a Best steam tractor. Mill founder Art Thatcher is sitting next to the smokestack. The Thatcher lumber mill near Viola was a true pioneer in the area's lumber business. To this day there is a Thatcher Lumber Company in Redding though the mill has long ceased operations. Courtesy, Marjorie Thatcher Beeman*

ker Hill mining operation.

Oddly enough, while Redding in later years became home to many local lumber industry officials—J.T. McDonald, A.B. Hood, William Main, and others—few big mills were built inside the city limits, despite the subsequent availability of inexpensive power from Shasta Dam. One reason perhaps was the city's beginning as a railhead, which attracted settlement close to the tracks. Another, no doubt, was taxes. Some mills and remanufacturing centers were established just south of the city limits. A few sawmills were also located north of the city in the Central Valley area. One early lumber plant occupied the site where the civic auditorium now stands. But the giant mills of the industry's early days in Shasta County were clustered around Anderson, ten miles to the south.

Redding's growth and the mining industry boosted the lumber economy during its early years. Timber was needed for the vertical shafts that brought up ore from the different mine levels, and for shoring up tunnels dug to ore deposits. Boards were required for the hast-

ily constructed saloons, hotels, livery stables, ware-
houses, and shops of the mining towns that sprang up
around Redding.

Lumbering sparked such eastern county settlements
as Round Mountain, Montgomery Creek, Buzzard's
Roost, Viola, Shingletown, and Manton. A flour mill to
feed the hungry lumberjacks and miners formed the basis for Buncombe, a community that later became Millville.

The Thatcher Lumber Company was started after
Ezekiel Thatcher settled on Bear Creek to the west of
Millville. The first sawmill was built in Millville in
1850 or 1851. Tom Thatcher, Ezekiel's grandson, said
his grandfather "hauled the first load of lumber out of
the mountains with three yoke of oxen." Rudolph
Klotz, who later served in the state assembly, also
founded an early sawmill in eastern Shasta County
near Shingletown.

The Terry Lumber Company was among the first to
establish a direct line operation from the logging woods
to the railroad and markets outside the county. The
company built a sawmill near Round Mountain and a

Above: *These loggers take time from their day's work for the Terry Lumber Company to enjoy a midday meal. The surroundings were less than fancy but the food was wholesome and plentiful. Clean hands were not required. Courtesy, Shasta Historical Society*

Right: *These folks are posing for a photograph in celebration of the Sacramento Valley and Eastern Railroad's completion in 1908. The railroad ran from Pit Station to Bully Hill, servicing mining operations. The wooden bridge was later replaced by a metal one; the site today lies beneath Shasta Lake. Courtesy, Charlotte Engle*

Opposite page: *The Terry Lumber Company Flume was an awesome sight standing high above treetops and spanning wide canyons. Built to transport cut lumber from the sawmill in Round Mountain to the planing mill and distribution yards in Bella Vista, the flume traversed approximately thirty miles of rough terrain. Courtesy, Elwood and Lucile Ward*

twenty-eight-mile wooden flume to carry lumber to a remanufacturing plant at Bella Vista, just east of Redding, so it could be planed, graded, and sent to market. A narrow-gauge railroad was built to Anderson over what is now Deschutes Road to carry the finished product to the main line where it could be switched to larger cars and sent to the sales distribution yard in Red Bluff.

A railroad engine that was used to pull the lumber fell into the Sacramento River near the present Deschutes Road bridge east of Anderson. A contractor's effort to locate it in the river's depths during bridge construction several years ago was unsuccessful.

Logging and woodworking industries also flourished in the shadow of towering Lassen Peak, still a sleeping volcano in the late 1800s. B.F. Loomis, who later became famous for his photos of volcanic eruptions, built a water-powered sawmill near Viola.

Because of the rigors of early lumbering and market uncertainties, the work attracted mostly single men. They lived in camps, slept in rude wooden "muzzle-loader" bunks in bunkhouses, and often worked from sunup to sundown to harvest as many trees as possible during the dry weather. Higher echelon employees could afford to marry and the owners themselves often lived in baronial splendor, fashioning small mansions from their own lumber.

There is one story that Buzzard's Roost near Round Mountain was so named because of the lonely men who sat on rail fences to visit with each other on Sunday mornings. Roy Wilsey, an early-day resident, offered

another explanation. He said the place got its name from drunken loggers leaning over the rails to rid themselves of bad booze encountered during weekend celebrations.

The younger lumberjacks found many outlets for their frustrations. On Saturday nights they forsook the tame life of camp for the entertainment bistros of Redding, sometimes walking both ways for the opportunity. Redding's proximity to the mines and mills encouraged another trade, which brazen young women plied with abandon in the trackside rooming houses along California Street.

There are tall tales of daring young men who rode the lumber rafts down the flume to spend their wildness in Redding, returning with the freight wagons that brought materials and supplies for the camps. But Wilsey, who worked on the flume as a teenager, doesn't mention that risky form of transportation in his 1971 book, *Hillbilly Boy;* he does, however, devote an entire chapter to the flume itself.

A grand contrivance when it was built, the flume had trestles as high as 120 feet spanning ravines and gorges. The product of shade-tree carpenters, it was a construction marvel that existed despite timber jams, huge leaks, and other complications until the 1920s, when it fell prey to age, weather, and disrepair, and was abandoned. Today, not a trace of the old flume remains. Farmers removed some of the boards for barns and fences; wildfires took the rest.

As forests were cut away from the sawmills, moving the logs to sawmills became harder. Oxen were used at

first, their strength as hefty with log wagons as with the lurching prairie schooners. Huge wagon wheels and steam tractors next provided the mobility needed to bring logs to sawmills. The wheels had sturdy wooden spokes. When pulled by a tractor, a pair could carry a brace of logs over rough terrain by dragging the smaller ends, butts cinched tightly beneath the wheel's axle.

The industry grew in spurts during the early 1900s. The San Francisco earthquake of 1906 created a sudden demand for lumber. Lumber mills and plants prospered from construction demands for barracks and wartime housing during World Wars I and II. A big demand followed the Second World War as returning GIs came home to set up housekeeping.

Anderson-area mills were influenced by the fabulous Red River Lumber Company, focus of the T.B. Walker timber interests, which at one time had one of the largest pine mills in the world at Westwood in Lassen County. When the mill closed down in the 1940s as a result of poor markets and obsolescence, it freed a shelf of timber on the west side of Lassen Peak for market-

Above: This circa 1918 view of Redding, looking north from West Street near Gold Street, indicates that the lumber industry had a ready market among the city's early homeowners. The square steeple of St. Joseph Catholic Church appears in the left and the Lorenz Hotel is in the distance. Courtesy, Veronica Satorius

Above Left: This photo, taken in 1946 at McCloud Flat on the lower slopes of Mt. Shasta, shows a crew loading a truck with a one-log load. That one ponderosa pine log contained over 5,000 board feet of lumber and was all the truck could haul. The crew and equipment were part of the J.J. Bartle Logging Company of Fall River Mills. Courtesy, John and Rose Bartle and the Fort Crook Historical Society

Opposite page: "Donkey Engines," wood-burning, steam-powered winches mounted on heavy wooden skids, were used to drag sectioned logs to a central landing for loading onto wagons or a logging railroad. The engines generally had a four-man crew composed of an operator, fireman, "whistle punk," and "wood buck." Others called "choker setters" would, with the help of horses, drag the long cables and attach them to the felled log sections. Courtesy, Tom and Frances Dunlap

The Ralph L. Smith Lumber Company, established along the rail-road tracks just south of Anderson, was just one lumber company developed in the county during the post-World War II boom years. Courtesy, Redding Museum and Art Center

ing. As a result, the Ralph L. Smith Lumber Company, the Paul Bunyan Lumber Company, and others were established in Shasta County in the boom years that followed World War II.

North of Anderson, almost midway to Redding beside then Highway 99, an obscure plywood company—then little more than a hole-in-the-wall office in New York's financial district—purchased an existing plywood plant. The new company had the pretentious name of U.S. Plywood Corporation and a daring idea: set up a particleboard plant to make a product out of chip by-products of lumber using pressed-wood manufacturing processes.

U.S. Plywood management teamed Warren Smith, a company engineer, with a Swiss inventor named Fred Fahrni, who had produced such a board through home research. Smith visited Fahrni at his home in Europe and the product "Novoply" was born. Fahrni supervised construction of the plant in the growing U.S. Plywood complex. The future looked bright.

Manufacture of Novoply enhanced the company's output and sales increased. Plant manager Gene Brewer of Redding was promoted to corporation president. Growth and mergers followed until more than 100 plants across the nation were in the corporate fold. Success led to a merger and takeover by Champion In-

ternational and the Plywood name receded into the background.

But Novoply's bloom carried seeds of disaster. Shortly after midnight on a spring night in 1976 a dust explosion sent a fiery ball of fury through the factory. It caused a second, greater blast and the huge plant became an inferno. Valiant efforts by firefighters managed to save adjoining buildings. The disaster claimed nine lives and caused an estimated twenty-five million dollars in damages.

For several years, Champion officials were beset by lawsuits and investigations. Insurance companies paid off seven million dollars in claims. A settlement was finally reached after fourteen lawsuits were consolidated into one in Shasta County Superior Court and heard before Judge Richard Abbe. It resulted in two-and-a-half million dollars being paid to relatives and heirs of the victims.

The Novoply plant was never rebuilt, and without it the Champion plant never recovered. Without Novoply it was thrown to the mercies of the mercurial lumber and plywood markets. Prolonged recession in the early 1980s and a complex merger with the St. Regis Corporation led to the plant's closure in 1984.

Other lumber plants also felt the pain of recession. By Redding's centennial year, its civic leaders were openly wondering what kind of future was in store for the wood products industry.

It wasn't always thus. When the so-called "Baby Boomers," the bumper crop of infants born in the 1940s and 1950s, reached maturity, they added new fuel to a lumber boom already beset by inflation and its effects. Real estate values soared as speculative home buyers found riches in quick turnovers for profit. It seemed as if the good times would never end.

Federal foresters felt the pressure to put more timber on the market from national forests. One-fourth of the money earned from timber sales was returned to counties for use on roads and schools. And since timber bid prices were pegged to prevailing market rates of lumber, companies could readily find margins for operating costs.

In the midst of this came the Kimberly-Clark Corporation of Neenah, Wisconsin, which brought papermaking to the scene. With the advent of Kimberly Clark, the lumber industry prospered during the late 1960s and early 1970s.

Kimberly-Clark purchased the Ralph L. Smith complex near Anderson and persuaded county officials through a series of often controversial hearings to allow it to build a kraft pulp mill there. The corporation officials promised the mill would be of the latest design and compatible with fish and wildlife of the Sacramento River. Company president John Kimberly and his invited guest, Governor Edmund G. "Pat" Brown, Sr., toured the new facility after dedication ceremonies in June 1964.

Though the plant made itself known through sometimes noxious odors, Kimberly-Clark proved to be a good neighbor. When the company decided to sell its interests in the early 1970s, Simpson Lee Paper Company and Roseburg Lumber Company purchased the pulp and paper and woodworking plants, respectively. Simpson Lee (now Simpson) added cogeneration facilities for electricity in the early 1980s. Roseburg eventually closed its acquired sawmill in Mt. Shasta, but has continued to operate in the Anderson plant.

While the industry became a wheelhorse of the county's economy, signs of trouble were appearing. Companies found it more and more difficult to meet inflated prices of federal timber. Operating costs continued to increase.

Massive strikes that included Redding mills paralyzed the industry in the Northwest as operators tried to hold the line against wage demands brought by inflation-hurt workers.

Bid practices led companies to offer higher and higher amounts for federal timber even as logging and transportation costs increased. Environmental factors also restricted logging and added to timber costs.

Logging and lumber methods were changing, too. Sawmills that once employed hundreds of men began cutting back as push-button automation took over production. The changes freed workers from menial tasks, but many also lost their jobs.

During the early 1980s, the great green crescent of forests around Redding's northern perimeter still seemed serene and aloof. But the giant firs and pines were gone, logged over the years and replaced by younger, less marketable growth.

Other industries and foreign competition also were making inroads on the once proud industry. Light metal mobile homes and prefabricated houses were gaining ground in a market that once seemed infallible for fixed-base homes. Lumber became decorative to steel-ribbed and concrete office buildings and condominiums. In south Redding, Eastside Road, once called "lumber row" because of its solid brace of remanufacturing plants, became diversified with other industries, service shops, and convenience stores.

The forest products industry crashed to earth in the early 1980s, falling like a lightning-struck snag and sending shock waves through the Redding business community.

Suddenly, big mills were closing and sending valued employees to the jobless rolls. They included International Paper Company of Weed, Plywood-Champion's mill at McCloud and eventually its complex at Anderson, and later, for a time, the Louisiana-Pacific Corporation mill at Burney. Unemployment rates climbed above 10 percent and stayed there in Shasta, Trinity, and Siskiyou counties.

To meet the crisis, the Redding business community redoubled its efforts to attract other types of industry. Some disappointed merchants predicted that the lumber industry was down for the count and that the county's future lay in other diversified industry and recreation.

Others, though, saw the industry as only being in a trough while it retooled and reshaped its destiny to meet the demands of an increasingly competitive market.

*McCloud was established in the late 1800s, in the shadow of Mt.
Shasta. It survived quite well on the timber industry until the late
1970s when the industry declined. Since then the town has been
struggling with sawmill closures and a dwindling population. Photo
by Scott Nystrom.* Courtesy, Record Searchlight

Recreation
Brings People

The mantle of outdoor recreation, as wide as the green forests that frame Shasta Lake, brought Redding its latest—and some say, greatest—"golden crescent."

The city became a tourist center by a happy coincidence of circumstances and events. Mt. Shasta, Lassen Peak, and the Trinity Alps, however peripheral to Redding itself, were already in the region or its vicinity. As for events, the railroad had arrived, Shasta and Trinity dams had been built, air travel was expanded, and improved communications was developing.

The state needed power and water for its thirsty southland with its teeming cities. The north had both in untapped resources. Central California also needed safety from rampaging winter floods as well as avenues of escape from metromania. What better way to complement flood control, power development, and water conservation than with tourism and outdoor recreation?

Even prior to Shasta Dam, the north state's recreational potential was becoming recognized in the rest of the state. The Southern Pacific touted the beauties of the Cascades in its promotional material for train rides through the Sacramento River Canyon.

Adventurous men like famed naturalist John Muir climbed Mt. Shasta, claimed by Redding as a tourist attraction although it was actually in neighboring Siskiyou County. Shasta and Trinity national forests were formed in 1905.

The Baird Caves, forerunner of Lake Shasta Caverns, inspired the curious and challenged spelunkers. Fishermen as famous as Theodore Roosevelt and

Shasta Lake, with its 365 miles of shoreline and vast surface area, has become the "houseboat capital" of Northern California. Water sports of all types have given the lake a reputation for year-round enjoyment. Courtesy, John Reginato, Shasta Cascade Wonderland Association

Above, right, and opposite page: *These B.F. Loomis photographs are those he took in succession during a Lassen Peak eruption on June 14, 1914. Courtesy, National Park Service*

Trinity Lake, behind Trinity Dam, offers some of the best and least populated fishing and boating in the state. Located fifty miles northeast of Redding in Trinity County, the area is missed by the majority of recreation seekers. Photo by Scott Nystrom. Courtesy, Record Searchlight

Herbert Hoover dipped hooks in the Sacramento, Pit, and Klamath rivers.

Resort hotels sprang up almost as soon as the railroad punched through the canyon, some beginning as stagecoach stops even before the trains. Among the more famous was Southern's resort hotel in the Sacramento River Canyon north of Redding. Built by a veteran Shasta hotel man, Southern's boasted among its guests of the late 1880s President Rutherford B. Hayes and General William T. Sherman.

Lassen Volcanic National Park became a tourist attraction after it was formed by an act of Congress in 1916, the result of a series of eruptions that began in May 1914. Although sharing access with Anderson, Chico, and Red Bluff, the park nevertheless brought overnight visitors to Redding. The B.F. Loomis Museum, with its photos of earlier Lassen Peak eruptions, was a popular park attraction until it was ordered closed during the 1970s after geologists warned that the museum's vicinity was prone to danger from landslides.

In Redding itself, people took their recreation where they could find it. The Diestelhorst resort was a popular spa in summer during the 1930s and 1940s. It stood near the antique Diestelhorst Bridge, a concrete trough which spans the river to the north and still carries traffic. Some fine times were had at affairs held by the Diestelhorst sisters. Mabel and Isobel Diestelhorst never married and after they died their brother George sold the property to the city, which disposed of the building.

Swimming holes were at a premium in summer because of the heat. Residents otherwise sought ingenious ways just to keep cool. During really hot days, old-time residents soaked sheets and tented them over beds and other havens of rest. Outdoors, the sheets were thoroughly soaked and draped around trees to form cones.

In summer the richer residents spirited their families away to higher elevations, where the breadwinners joined them on weekends. Later, as the automobile shortened distances, the sojourns were made nightly.

Opposite page: *Lake Shasta Caverns are truly one of nature's won-* *ders. The caverns are within a massive limestone outcropping on the* *McCloud arm of Shasta Lake visible from Interstate 5. For centuries* *an integral part of Wintu Indian lore, the caverns had their first re-* *corded visit by white men when James A. Richardson signed his* *name inside the caverns in 1878. Note the lone person standing high* *among the stalactites in the center of the photo. Courtesy, Lake* *Shasta Caverns*

Above: *In 1934 Redding built this swimming area on the Sacramento* *River east of the Diestelhorst Bridge using WPA "free" labor. The* *facility on the river's north bank was never a success. The current* *was too swift and cold for pleasant swimming and just six years af-* *ter completion the raging flood of 1940 undermined much of the new* *concrete. Courtesy, Vivian Harrigan*

Above: *The sun sets over a tranquil Shasta Lake. Photo by Tom Dunlap. Courtesy,* Record Searchlight

Opposite page: *This 1984 photo shows Achomawi fish traps built of lava rock at Crystal Springs near the Tule River. Ahjumawi Lava Springs State Park in eastern Shasta County was established in 1974. The 6,000-acre park is a haven for fish and wildlife plus Indian artifacts and sacred places of the Achomawi people. The word "Ahjumawi" translates as "where the waters come together"; within the park, the Tule River, Little Tule River, Big Lake, and many springs converge. Photo by Tom Dunlap. Courtesy,* Record Searchlight

Recreation didn't really come into its own as a viable industry in Shasta County until the filling of Shasta Lake. Soon after, the Forest Service began issuing permits for resorts along the new shore of the man-made reservoir. The first resorts were rudimentary affairs. Dick Strandlund, among the first lakeside resort owners, recalled that some were little more than collections of outbuildings and shacks.

But it was soon discovered that the lake's glassy summer surface was ideal for waterskiing. After that, other forms of relaxation weren't far in tow. Boaters, campers, and fishermen began swarming to the new lake.

The lake's potential for recreation led Charles J. Gleeson, former managing editor of the *Record Searchlight,* to return to Redding and become manager of the Shasta Dam Area Chamber of Commerce in 1956. Gleeson managed the chamber until his retirement in 1976. He put together an organization that dovetailed the kindred ambitions of Central Valley business operators with those of lakeside resort owners. The chamber became a vocal supporter of recreation as a component of federal policies for administering Shasta Dam.

Even after the arrival of air conditioning, many ventured into the heat to share in water sports and other diversions. Shasta, Trinity, and Whiskeytown lakes

Located on the east side of Market Street south of the new city hall, Wright's Garage, the first of its kind in Redding, opened its doors for business in 1908. The owner, James D. Wright, was a former machinist with the Mountain Copper Company. Courtesy, Ray and Rika Coffelt

added hundreds of liquid acres to a water storage inventory that already included Lake Britton near Burney and other reservoirs.

Shasta Lake's configuration enhanced the hamlet of Lakehead, and brought some of the lake's first resorts to an area on the Sacramento arm called Sugarloaf. The lake also created islands and boat-access campgrounds. One of the more famous is the Kamloops campground, where sportsmen's groups Kamloops Incorporated and Steelhead Unlimited meet annually in June for a weekend of fishing, camping, and tall tales.

Recreation in the area has had its champions. Among the more colorful was the late Henry "Hank" Clineschmidt, the son of Temple Hotel owners, who served nine years on the state Fish and Game Commission. Clineschmidt has been credited with organizing

Left: *Henry Erle "Hank" Clineschmidt was born in Redding in 1912. His grandfather bought the Temple Hotel in 1894 (for $26,000) and Clineschmidt owned the hotel for forty years. The founding president of California Kamloops, Inc. in 1950, he also founded Steelhead Unlimited, Inc. in 1952. He served on the state Fish & Game Commission from 1959 until 1968 and died in 1982. Courtesy, Shasta Cascade Wonderland Association*

Below: *Here, Dunsmuir celebrates its 100th birthday in 1986. Born as a railhead, it thrived until the decline of steam locomotives in the late 1940s and early 1950s. Today the community, fifty-two miles north of Redding near Mt. Shasta, is developing into a mecca of outdoor recreation. Photo by Tom Dunlap. Courtesy, Record Searchlight*

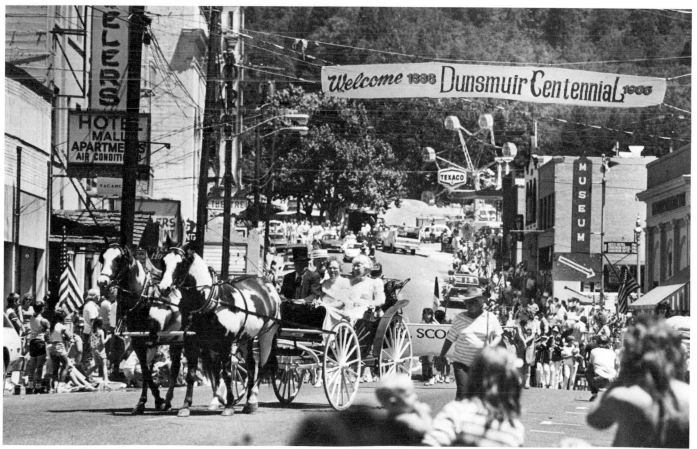

the Kamloops Incorporated and Steelhead Unlimited, groups dedicated to stocking game fish in Shasta and other lakes, streams, and tributaries of the Sacramento River.

John Reginato, another north state champion of recreation, was still on the job in 1986 after thirty-eight years as manager of the Redding-based multi-county Shasta Cascade Wonderland Association.

The growth of recreation in Shasta County would have been difficult without the advent of modern forms of transportation and communication. As the area developed, mule travel gave way to train travel, which in turn gave way to automobiles, while former stagecoach and freight wagon roads became paved highways. Narrow, two-lane ribbons of asphalt at first, they were improved over the years to meet the area's increasingly mobile demands for outdoor pleasure.

People wanted to reach vacation haunts quickly and gain as many hours of leisure as possible. A "short cut" need for weekend gamblers from Oregon and the North State to Reno led Highway 89's development from a point south of Burney to Susanville.

To make travel easier, torturous mountain roads were rebuilt, like Highway 299 west over Buckhorn Summit to Weaverville which cost as much as one million dollars per mile. By 1968, a full thirty years after the start of Shasta Dam, Highway 99 had been rebuilt into the federal interstate system as Interstate 5 from Churn Creek north of Redding to the northern shore of Shasta Lake. The freeway was extended through the Enterprise area (now Redding) and past Anderson by 1970.

Herbert Miles, then the state's district highway engineer, predicted the freeway would extend from Canada

Opposite page: *This 1928 photograph shows Anton Schwegerl stand-ing beside a Shell Oil truck he drove throughout the region to supply the needs of a new motorized economy. Logging, mining, and agricul-ture plus newcomers, tourism, and recreation put added demands on the amount of fuel needed. Courtesy, Shasta Historical Society*

Above: *Heavy wooden forms were built in 1916 for the construction of the concrete bridge across the Pit River to carry traffic on the new "highway" going north which later became U.S. Highway 99. Today the bridge still stands, submerged beneath the waters of Shasta Lake just east of the I-5 bridge at Bridge Bay. Courtesy, Shasta Historical Society*

Aircraft were a most unusual sight around Redding in the early 1900s. When this primitive biplane landed in town as part of the 1909 Air Show, it drew a large crowd of curious spectators. Courtesy, Shasta Historical Society

to Mexico by 1972 "if everyone keeps up their end of the bargain." But the credit crunch and oil crisis of the mid-1970s delayed some portions indefinitely. As 1985 ended, the state was still awaiting funds to complete a final portion of freeway north of Lakehead.

Aircraft first appeared in Redding in 1908, according to Henry "Hank" Woodrum, retired city airports manager. Two pilots used the north end of Court Street as a runway only five years after the Wright Brothers made aviation history at Kitty Hawk in 1906.

Charles Hamilton flew a Curtiss biplane over the county in 1911. The daring aviator appeared in Redding only five days after being scalded in a crash on a state fair racetrack.

The balloon *America* used the field successfully for a day or two before it exploded and burned in midair over Redding on July 3, 1909, during a Fourth of July

Possibly the first air show ever held in Redding played host to disaster. On July 3, 1909, as the zeppelin Airship America was ascending before a large crowd, the propeller somehow came in contact with the balloon itself at a height of approximately fifty feet. The zeppelin exploded into flames and the pilot was killed. Courtesy, Shasta Historical Society

celebration.

As late as the mid-1920s, an assortment of aircraft landed on an east-west strip just south of Benton Drive where a golf course and railroad trestle are now. They included Jennys flown by pilots selling rides.

Two Jennys landed in 1917, the first military aircraft to set down in Shasta County, part of a flight of three from Eureka (the other flew back to that city). One Jenny pilot made a forced landing in a Happy Valley stubble field and the other pilot landed to help him repair the craft.

A Redding committee formed to develop an airport, and eventually purchased land adjacent to Placer Road just west of town in 1927. The committee paid $8,500 for 451 acres and established Benton Field, dedicating it in 1929 ceremonies to the memory of Lieutenant John Benton, a Redding native and one of two West

Coast army pilots selected for a good will flight to South America. He was killed in a crash at Buenos Aires on that flight.

Benton's runway lengths were not sufficient for larger aircraft and so city officials began promoting an airport on the Stillwater Plains during the 1930s. The project was delayed during 1939 to 1940 but expedited in 1941 after the Japanese attack on Pearl Harbor. Redding Municipal Airport was completed in May 1942 and was used during the war as a squadron base for P-39s that summer. It was used as an auxiliary field the rest of the war. The county's interest in the airport was acquired by Redding in 1947 which since has developed it into a modern facility with a control tower and accommodations for jet airliners. In recent years it has become the scene of an annual air show.

In the 1960s Benton Field survived a bitter election campaign brought on by a civic faction that wished to have the field sold to a subdivider. It was since renamed Benton Airpark and is used mostly by pilots of smaller aircraft.

Whether traveling by air or road, visitors to the area have been beckoned by natural attractions in the hinterlands.

Nourished by snow-fed Burney Creek, Burney Falls, which drops 129 feet, was once called by Theodore Roosevelt the "eighth wonder of the world."

Burney Falls has beckoned visitors since the first settlers arrived. It was deeded to the state by Frank and Ethel McArthur (descendants of the 1869 Pit River settler, John McArthur,) in 1930 and became the centerpiece of McArthur-Burney Falls State Park, one of the oldest parks in the state system.

The McArthurs deeded 160 acres and the state added 175 acres in a purchase three years later. They were descendants of John McArthur, who settled along the Pit River in 1869.

North of Redding, skiing became popular during the 1960s when Redding financiers Carl and Leah McConnell rescued the floundering Mt. Shasta Ski Bowl and its 1,400 stockholders with a financial transfusion of $600,000. Later, the city and the *Record Searchlight* sponsored ski lessons at the resort for several years. The memorable winter of 1968 to 1969 brought snow of incredible depths to the mountain but failed to stop the skiing. The resort met a Waterloo fate several years later, however, when an avalanche swept away a ski tow facility.

Above: *Carl McConnell was a Redding entrepreneur and philanthropist who financed the first ski resort on Mt. Shasta. He passed away February 19, 1985, leaving a legacy that included a foundation for helping the Redding community. Photo by Tom Dunlap. Courtesy, Record Searchlight*

Above, left: *In this 1916 view looking north up Market Street from Placer Street, a surface of gravel and oil is being laid. Glover's Garage is on the left, while McCormick-Saeltzer's "big store" is across Placer Street beside smoking equipment. Courtesy, Maida Glover Gandy*

A plan to rebuild the ski facility at a lower elevation became mired in controversy when conservationist groups protested that it would despoil prime wilderness. Usage versus wilderness continued for several years until the controversy finally was resolved in 1985 in legislation developed by Senator Peter Wilson (R-California).

Communications in Redding began in a rudimentary fashion with homegrown experiments in establishing telephone lines. Pacific Bell records show that local telephone service was established as early as 1881. It was primitive at best, with early lines strung between homes and businesses. The first to have one was Captain Charles E. Berry, a local tinsmith, who set up a line between his shop and house. The voice boxes were made of tin (Berry's own idea) and the lines were of copper, attached to convenient trees and houses. Berry called his invention "The Boss."

Berry's invention led to other telephones over the next few years. By 1890 wire replaced the more primitive materials of rawhide and sheepskin; by 1894 negotiations had begun with Sunset Telephone Company of San Francisco, a forerunner of Ma Bell. The city granted the company a twenty-five-year franchise.

Eaton's Drug Store had the first central switchboard, with Villa Thompson as the first operator. She worked a ten-hour day for fifteen dollars a month. By 1898 a long-distance line destined to link San Francisco and Portland reached Redding. That same year the *Daily Free-Press* started a "News by Telephone" column.

While telephone communication came early in Redding's history, mass electronic communication didn't really arrive until after World War II, when radio and television came to the fore. By 1960 Redding had a local television station and several radio stations. Two evolved during the 1970s through some changes of ownership into KQMS radio and KRCR-TV, Channel 7R among private broadcsters. Public broadcasting was developed through a unique nine-county station called KIXE-TV, Channel 9. Meanwhile, a newcomer has appeared on the scene; KCPM-Channel 24, started programming on an ultra-high frequency signal in September 1985 as an NBC affiliate in Redding and Chico.

These communications and transportation improvements, along with the creation of new lakes and resort facilities, launched the region into a prime recreation area. Governor George Deukmejian's administration has encouraged the area's tourism industry by promoting national recognition through various communications media. And in April 1986 Rand McNally & Co. the world's largest travel guide publisher and mapmaker, rated the area the nation's best spot for "Blessings of Nature."

Above: *This is Mt. Shasta Ski Park as it appeared on its opening day in 1985. The new facility offers two lifts, classes, equipment rentals, and a lodge. In the distance is the snow-capped peak of Mt. Shasta. Photo by Tom Dunlap. Courtesy,* Record Searchlight

Opposite page: *Lassen Park Ski Area is located near Mineral at the southwest entrance to Lassen Volcanic National Park. The ski area offers lodge and lift facilities and is a regional attraction to ski enthusiasts. Photo by Tim Dunn. Courtesy,* Record Searchlight

Centennial
—in the Sun—

The Redding of the twentieth century was scarcely on the minds of a small group of men who met on the evening of October 10, 1887, in the office of attorney W.D. Biegle to chart the course of the six-day-old city. They were practical individuals who sensed that their community was at a crossroads—either it would go forward or wither and die like Shasta, its predecessor to the west. They had no way of foreseeing the industrial, commercial, and recreational center the city was to become.

Since Shasta Dam's construction, the region has been blessed with a coalition of talented men and women who managed the county in a manner that would have made the original developers proud.

There was the indomitable J.S. "Sid" Cowgill, chamber manager from 1963 to 1975, who literally lived and died for Redding, working until ill health compelled his early retirement shortly before his death. Cowgill is remembered by some Redding residents for his jaunty personality, as he made his rounds of downtown businesses with his little dog, "Pin-Pin."

During Cowgill's tenure, plans were initiated for the civic auditorium, the state was persuaded to widen the two-lane Cypress Avenue Bridge across the Sacramento River to four lanes, and the downtown mall began development.

Cowgill also led the first effort to annex the Enterprise area to Redding in 1963. It failed at the polls in a flurry of last-minute charges by opponents. Among the backers of that ill-fated proposal was Fred W. Marler, Jr., a Redding attorney who became a state senator from Shasta and Trinity counties and later a Sacramento superior court judge.

A later annexation measure fared better. It was approved by voters of the city and Enterprise Public

Whiskeytown Lake offers the best sailing conditions in the Redding area. Besides sailboarding, popular sports are water skiing, fishing, camping, swimming, canoeing, and hiking. Photo by Tom Dunlap. Courtesy, Record Searchlight

Above: *As the town of Redding grew and prospered, old institutions gave way to new. In 1959 the southwest corner of Market and Placer streets was dominated by Woolworth's, while next door is the once thriving operation of Glover's automobile service garage. Today, the garage is gone and so too Woolworth's. Courtesy, Maida Glover Gandy*

Right: *Virgil Covington managed a lumber planing mill in Anderson owned by his father, served in Anderson city government, and in 1965 headed the Economic Development Corporation (EDC) of Shasta County, until his death in 1982. Photo by Tom Dunlap. Courtesy, Record Searchlight*

Utility District in 1976, following hard on the heels of annexation of the Cascade Community Services District. Both mergers swelled the city's population from less than 17,000 to more than 44,000.

As the city grew, it spread east across the river, taking in the higher ground of Enterprise when the annexation became official in December 1976, and moving into the western foothills in the years following. It snaked into canyons south of town, and occupied the bluffs north of the river with the boom times of Shasta Dam. It spread subdivisions as far south as Clear Creek and the former site of old Horsetown, and west almost to old Shasta itself during the 1970s. Its population expanded, along with the county's. In 1960 the total county census figure was 49,468. Ten years later it had climbed to 77,640, and by 1980 it was 115,715.

The first city manager was George T. Charles. His successor was Phil W. Storm, who served from April 1947 until 1952. Storm later became city manager of Avalon, Buena Park, and Cupertino. He died in 1985 in Reno.

A successsion of managers followed. Among them were Robert W. Cowden (who left Redding to serve as city manager of several cities) and Bill Brickwood, now both retired and living in Redding, and Robert Courtney, the present manager and former finance director who plans to retire in 1987.

Another civic dynamo was Maurice "Moe" Finn, a feisty but genial labor leader who came to town to organize a union of hospital workers and remained to become the first manager of the city's new civic auditorium. Finn won legions of friends and the community's respect with a combination of Irish wit and dogged determination, spreading his influence by sheer dint of personality.

His recommendation by Cowden to manage the new auditorium drew some criticism among conservatives because of his labor background, but he proved to be an able manager, attracting several major conventions to Redding and serving until his death from cancer a few years later.

Virgil Covington, a former Anderson mayor and Trinity County lumberman, managed the fledgling Economic Development Corporation of Shasta County in the 1960s. He made it a showcase agency for economic development, creating Redding's Mountain Lakes Industrial Park on the city's northern outskirts.

There have been others in passing, too numerous to

John Sidney Cowgill piloted the Redding Chamber of Commerce from 1963 until 1975. Photo by Charles Miller. Courtesy, Record Search-light

117

mention, among them Vern Speer, outspoken publisher of a business weekly; Judge Joseph Aleck, caustic iconoclast of the Redding justice court; and big-hearted Supervisor John Strange, who never hesitated to help someone in distress.

As Redding changed from a "masculine" economy—dependent on lumber, mining, construction, and agriculture—to a trade, tourism, and cultural center, women came to the fore in more trades and professions, and emerged as prominent county leaders.

One woman who was a major contributor to county government was Lucy Hunt, who served as the county superintendent of schools for twenty years until her retirement on January 1, 1963. A graduate of San Jose State College, she previously taught in sixteen schools throughout California. At one time she supervised fifty elementary school districts in the county, almost twice as many as today.

Esther Mardon, the county's first librarian, was a feisty champion for one's right to knowledge, never hesitating to take on county supervisors or anyone else. After her retirement she was a prime mover in the establishment of the Friends of the Shasta County Libraries in 1980.

Successful professional women include Marie Whitacre, who, in 1986, headed the Shasta County Board of Realtors, and Patsy Ernst, who headed the Redding branch of Crocker National Bank.

Yet not until 1972 did the Shasta County Board of Supervisors have a female member, when Bessie Sanders of Shasta succeeded retiring John Perez, himself a champion of county water development. Mrs. Sanders completed two terms as supervisor of the county's District Two in 1980. She was board chairwoman twice, in 1975 and 1979. In 1976 she chaired the county's Bicentennial Committee. During her tenure, she played a lead role in developing more extensive county-wide fire protection and animal control, chaired a nine-county committee on water development, and fostered preservation of historical documents.

Right, above: *Barbara Gard was elected Redding's first city councilwoman in 1976 and first woman mayor in 1982. She was a delegate to the Democratic National Convention in San Francisco in 1984. Photo by Tom Dunlap. Courtesy,* Record Searchlight

Right: *Bessie Sanders became Shasta County's first woman supervisor when elected in 1972. She served as such until her retirement in January 1981. Photo by Gary Miller. Courtesy,* Record Searchlight

The Carnegie Library, a quaint brick building facing Yuba Street, opened in 1903. The quiet was shattered periodically as steam locomotives thundered by on the rails just outside. The building was torn down in 1962 and the bricks were later used to cover the outside walls of the present police and city council building. Courtesy, Ray and Rika Coffelt

The male stronghold of city government fell to Barbara Gard, who became Redding's first councilwoman in 1976 and was reelected in 1980 and 1984. Gard served as mayor from April 1982 to April 1984, and has chaired the city's Parks and Recreation Commission, the Redding Museum and Art Center board, and the centennial planning committee.

A self-described "political junkie," Gard was a delegate to the 1984 Democratic convention in San Francisco, where she supported Geraldine Ferraro for vice-president.

Besides the primary economic base provided by mining, lumber, power, and recreation, the county has also been supported by strong secondary industries, among them health care and retirement.

From humble origins as St. Caroline Hospital, a wooden structure at Pine and Sacramento streets in the early 1900s, Mercy Medical Center has grown into a multimillion-dollar health care facility. Currently it is developing a four-story nursing tower and outpatient cancer center as the final phase of a $30-million expansion project due for completion in September 1988.

Downtown, the hospital that began as Dr. Thomas

Above: *This scene of abandoned ranch buildings is reminiscent of Redding's frontier past. Photo by Robert McKenzie*

Opposite page, top: *Redding Medical Center first opened its doors in 1945 under the name of Memorial Hospital. It changed its name to Redding Medical Center in 1981. Located at East and Tehama Streets in downtown Redding, the rapidly expanding facility recently completed a new three-story addition to increase its public services. Courtesy, Tom and Frances Dunlap*

Opposite page, bottom: *Mercy Medical Center traces its roots back to 1907 when it was founded at Pine and Sacramento streets using the name of Saint Caroline Hospital. In 1953 the Sisters of Mercy opened their new hospital at its present location in Clairmont Heights using the name Mercy Hospital. Today Mercy Medical Center is a leader in north state health care and continues to grow at a rapid rate. Photo by Tom Dunlap. Courtesy, Record Searchlight*

Right: *The rural lifestyle attracts many to Shasta County. This scene was captured near Ono. Photo by Robert W. Small*

Below: *The timber industry is still active in the Redding area. The man in the foreground of this logging crew is a "scaler"; he keeps track of the board-feet of lumber loaded onto each truck. Photo by Tom Dunlap*

Opposite page, top: *These fountains are on the grounds of the Redding Civic Auditorium and Civic Center. Photo by Tom Dunlap*

Opposite page, bottom: *The 1985 Rodeo Week parade was the biggest since the first Redding Rodeo in 1948. Trumpeter Andy Anderson and the West Valley High School marching band were one of the 200 parade entries. Photo by Tom Dunlap*

Above: *Looking across the Sacramento Canyon, photographer Robert McKenzie captured this view of Castle Crags.*

Opposite page, top: *Sailboat races are held every Memorial Day weekend on Whiskeytown Lake. The participants come from all over the West. Photo by Robert W. Small*

Opposite page, bottom: *Mt. Shasta reigns over this small lake perched at the top of Castle Crags. Photo by Robert McKenzie*

Right: *An angler enjoys a quiet afternoon of fishing on the Sacramento River near the Diestelhorst Bridge in Lake Redding Park. Photo by Tom Dunlap*

Below: *The "Three Shastas"—Shasta Dam, Shasta Lake, and Mt. Shasta—are a beautiful combination of man-made and natural splendor. Shasta Dam holds back the state's largest man-made reservoir. Photo by Robert W. Small*

Above: *Mt. Lassen and the Chaos Crags are reflected in the waters of Manzanita lake. Photo by Robert McKenzie*

Left: *The Ptotem Creek Falls, which falls into Shasta Lake, is inspiring aquatic sight. Photo by Robert McKenzie*

Wyatt's makeshift clinic, recently undertook a major expansion that included facilities for open-heart surgery. For many years known as Memorial Hospital, it became Redding Medical Center after it was taken over by National Medical Enterprises, Incorporated.

Shasta County's oldest hospital, Shasta General, is a modern accredited facility that includes a family practice unit in a sprawling medical complex in southeast Redding. In existence since 1855, the hospital has been situated in Redding since 1900. For many years a sanitarium for patients with tuberculosis was operated nearby, but with decline of the disease, it was converted to a county office building in the 1970s.

With growth of the three hospitals, other medical services have followed, such as eye clinics, prosthetics businesses, convalescent hospitals, holistic medical services, and retirement homes. In mid-1986 efforts were continuing to have an outpatient veterans clinic established in Redding.

Though the city was becoming a major medical community, trade center, and haven for the retired, Redding still didn't have a tie to a four-year institution of higher learning. A chamber study committee is presently studying the issue and trying to interest the Uni-

Above: Shasta Community College first opened its doors in September of 1950, and in June of 1951 held its first graduation ceremony, issuing eighteen diplomas. At that time the campus was adjacent to Shasta High School in Redding. In 1967 it moved to its present campus shown here at the intersection of Old Oregon Trail and Highway 299E. The 337-acre campus offers dormitories, a seventy-acre farm, shops and laboratories, a fire department and extensive athletic facilities. Courtesy, Shasta Community College

Above, right: Dr. Gilbert Collyer retired as Shasta College's first president in June of 1973. From an initial enrollment of 250, he guided the college's growth to become one with more than 10,000 students at the time of his retirement. Courtesy, Mary Nell Collyer

Opposite page: Cross-country skiing is enjoyed at Brokeoff Mountain in Lassen Park. Photo by Robert McKenzie

Right: *In this 1977 photograph, Loren L. Ewing is standing in front of Nova High School. The building was first opened for classes in 1927 and Ewing was among the new staff of charter teachers. The World War I veteran taught for many years in the Shasta Union High School District before his retirement. Photo by Tom Dunlap. Courtesy,* Record Searchlight

Below: *Redding Museum & Art Center is located in Caldwell Park on the bank of the Sacramento River. Containing exhibits of Native American culture as well as displays of pioneer life, the center exhibits contemporary art in two separate galleries. The Redding Museum is also the home of the Shasta Historical Society. Courtesy, Tom and Frances Dunlap*

versity of California and other institutions to locate in the community.

If the country has not yet laid claim to a four-year university, it has held Shasta College since 1950. The college owes much of its development to the late Dr. Gilbert A. Collyer, its president since the campus first opened its doors until his retirement in 1973.

The college began as a stepchild of the Shasta Union High School District, starting classes with 275 students. Collyer's main job was to design the first campus (now that of Shasta high School). He also traveled extensively in neighboring counties to recruit students.

Since 1963 the college has been governed by a district formed of portions of Shasta, Trinity, and Tehama counties. A new $12-million campus was completed on Stillwater Creek approximately six miles east of Redding in 1967.

By 1973 campus enrollment had grown to almost 10,000 students. The college had survived the turbulent 1960s with only a few skirmishes with students. Since the advent of Proposition 13, the main struggle

has been to balance budget cuts against educational needs.

As the county grew and matured, residents began taking an interest in the region's past and working to preserve its heritage. Toward that end, the Shasta Historical Society was organized in 1930. A nonprofit corporation since 1978, the society annually published the *Covered Wagon,* a booklet of accounts based upon research or personal recollection.

The Redding Museum and Art Center, another nonprofit corporation, was organized in 1963 to arrange exhibits, including historical displays, in cooperation with the historical society.

Mainly through the efforts of Carolyn Bond, its third and present director, the museum has grown into two separate buildings in Lake Redding Park.

One of the buildings, the Carter House Science Museum, was the home of a member of a remarkable family that produced two noted jurists, a beloved high school coach, and a current city councilman.

Jesse Carter became a state supreme court justice. Oliver Carter presided over the famed Patty Hearst

CARTER HOUSE SCIENCE MUSEUM

Carter House Science Museum is also located in Caldwell Park atop a knoll facing the Sacramento River. The displays and activities are geared for the enlightenment of the young though adults are always welcome. The museum is home for many species of birds, reptiles, and flora and fauna. Courtesy, Tom and Frances Dunlap

trial. Harlan Carter's service to Shasta High School caused the school to name Harlan Carter Gym in his memory. Scott Carter, a Shasta College instructor, was elected to the Redding City Council in 1986.

The city purchased the house in 1962 from Harlan Carter, who had built it twenty years earlier. In 1963 the historical society, an art federation, and an archaeological group combined forces to seek a museum site. The Carter House was made available and by 1973, using a combination of set-aside funds and federal restoration money, the new museum was ready to be built. It was dedicated on August 28, 1976.

Through the broad spectrum of history, Redding has developed from a turntable railroad town into a modern metropolitan center, while the county that nurtured it has changed from a regional montage of gritty mining, lumber, and construction scenes into an attractive landscape of man-made lakes freshening sparkling rivers and streams.

For a civic entity approaching its 100th birthday,

Redding seems amazingly spry and is looking quite confidently into the future. But the city is looking backward, too, and becoming more conscious of its origins as it approaches its centennial.

Redding has taken some recent hard knocks from a faltering lumber industry, but times are getting better again in the industry and it seems destined to prosper. Mining, too, is becoming active again after a relative dormancy of many years. Power and water exportation are basic industries that will continue to meet state-wide demands, while recreation and tourism should bring even more dollars to the area's economy in the years ahead.

But the mainstay of Redding can't be measured in dollars and cents or units of production. There is that unquenchable element of human spirit there that defies logic or explanation. I've tried to capture it by mentioning a few of the people who were inspired by it. For people make history, and Redding has had its share of movers and shakers.

If the county's past was somewhat lurid, this once young roughneck of a city is becoming mature and graceful now. Many of its shortcomings will probably be met by the year 2000. By then Redding should have a four-year university, stable employment, and a broad-based social, political, cultural, and economic structure. Based on present trends, the city should continue to develop as a regional center for manufacturing, services, and trade, expanding north toward Central Valley, east to Bella Vista and Palo Cedro, west to Shasta, and south as far as Anderson.

What has been good for Redding, for the most part, has been good for Anderson and Shasta County in general, even if the two cities and the county have not always seen eye to eye. Even in the early 1980s, a prolonged lawsuit over tax sharing held up development in the Canby Road, Mistletoe Lane, and Hilltop Drive areas of east Redding; in 1986 Redding and Anderson quarrelled over a site for a proposed sewer plant.

No matter, today's problems are often tomorrow's milestones of progress. From any vantage point the future of all three entities looks bright, and for this Redding and its builders can feel a great deal of pride.

As the city of Redding moves into its second century, it will increasingly dominate the north state, but it will be a benevolent influence, content to move at its own speed, and secure in the knowledge that the grim early days of "Poverty Flat" are no more.

Above: *Lou Gerard, Sr., will always be remembered as a true friend of Redding. He was active in many service organizations, including the Chamber of Commerce. He died July 19, 1986. Courtesy, Redding Elks Lodge 1073*

Opposite page: *Central Valley is a sprawling community bordered by smaller neighborhood communities such as Toyon, Project City, Pine Grove and Summit City. They all have a common heritage beginning with the construction of Shasta Dam almost fifty years ago. This view is down Shasta Dam Boulevard in the center of Central Valley Photo by Tom Dunlap. Courtesy,* Record Searchlight

Partners in Progress

Snow-topped Mt. Shasta to the north, Bully Choop Mountain to the west, and Lassen to the east look down on a thriving community in the northern end of the Sacramento-San Joaquin Valley.

Natural resources, abundant throughout the brief recorded history of Redding and Shasta County, and a strategic location provided the base for most of the community's growth and will continue to do so for generations to come, most analysts feel. In April 1986 this area was rated highest in the nation in "Blessings of Nature" by the world's largest travel guide publisher and map maker, Rand McNally & Co.

Gold, the precious yellow metal that spurred California's statehood, still lies hidden in the cracks and crevices of the nothern streams and mountains. Major Pierson B. Reading, Captain John Sutter's fur trapper, had been given a 26,000-acre Mexican land grant and established San Buena Ventura, with his home near what is now Cottonwood. When he heard reports of gold near Sacramento, he prospected there and touched off a local gold rush when he found the glitter nearby at what was to become Reading's Bar.

The railroad came to the "Queen City of the North" in the 1870s, moving quickly through the flat valley until it was slowed by the towering Cascades and faced an eleven-year effort to traverse the narrow, winding Sacramento River canyon. Much of the area's commerce was attributed to its location as the transportation keystone in all four directions, and business evolved around transshipment of goods from railroad to freight wagons.

Copper mining from the 1880s through World War I provided economic strength to the community but at an unacceptable price. The toxic smelter fumes denuded the hillsides for miles in all directions until the smelters were closed through legal action in the early 1900s.

Tourism began in a small way in the 1920s, but the Central Valley Project in 1938 initiated the construction of Shasta Dam and creation of Shasta Lake and later Whiskeytown Lake, today destination points for thousands of recreationists annually and dominant features in the Shasta County landscape.

Timber production from the bountiful forest dates back to the first settlers, but it wasn't until the early 1950s that the postwar building boom stimulated intensive harvesting. "Green gold" dominated the community for twenty years, and although now declined from its heyday, lumber production continues as the biggest single element in the economy with its future tied to professional management of some of the most productive timberlands in the world.

As the articles on the following pages illustrate, the businesses of Shasta County often had to struggle to become established elements of the community. But their success often evolved because they became a part of the community, giving back to that institution much of what they had received. Their support of a project such as this publication typifies the cooperative attitude that has seen Poverty Flat, as Redding was once called, evolve into the north state's economic keystone and the Gateway to the Cascades.

In the early 1920s the magic word was "electricity" both in the home as well as in industry. This battery shop in Redding was located at 1300 Market Street; the man in the foreground was probably Dan Briggs. Early batteries were cumbersome, dangerous, and toxic, but they were also necessary. Courtesy, Shasta Historical Society

GREATER REDDING AREA CHAMBER OF COMMERCE

In 1872 the Central Pacific Railroad arrived in what was then called Poverty Flats in Shasta County, several miles from the center of commerce at Shasta. There was no rational reason, at that time, for anyone to forsee the development of the City of Redding as the commercial hub that it has become. Similarly, there was little reason to expect that the railroad's program to sell off its land holdings would evolve into one of the most active chambers of commerce in California.

Initial commerce in Redding was to serve the needs of the railroad and those associated with it. The Central Pacific viewed agriculture as the future of the area and the railroad's promotional material related glowing tales to those in search of good farmland. But a series of droughts, food poisoning in locally canned olives, and severe pollution problems caused by the smelting industry diminished any potential boom in agriculture.

Until the turn of the century, business involvement in community development projects was rare except for mutual assistance with common problems such as fire and law enforcement. In the early 1900s, however, the chamber of commerce movement, which had burgeoned elsewhere, finally reached Northern California. Redding joined the movement of many small towns in efforts to stimulate trade, tourism, and economic development.

Although specific records are not available, it is generally believed that the Redding Chamber of Commerce was an outgrowth of the Shasta Development Association of the Central Pacific, and both groups shared the same office on Yuba Street between the Carnegie Library and the railroad track (now the parking lot behind the Lorenz Hotel).

Dudley Seltzer is credited with being the first president of the chamber, in 1910. On April 16, 1921, articles of incorporation for the Redding Chamber of Commerce were presented to the Secretary of State, with the ambitious, if generalized, goal "to promote the civic, economic, and social welfare of the people of Redding and vicinity," which today still serves as the guiding criteria for chamber activities.

The Greater Redding Area Chamber of Commerce boasts a membership of 1,200 and is supported by a professional staff of six full-time employees and an office located on Auditorium Drive near the Civic Auditorium. It concerns itself with nearly every major element of social and economic development in the community and operates without funds from any government source.

"While Redding has become the population, commercial, medical, and economic hub of far Northern California, our business and professional people still maintain the friendly, community-minded attitude so typical of smaller towns," says Lou Gerard, Jr., executive vice-president. "They give generously of their time and resources to support the community. The Jazz Festival, Small Business Week, Business Connection trade show, Chamberee, economic development programs, and some 24 working committees are the envy of many chambers. No other organization can equal the record of service or the ability to meet future challenges to make Redding a better place in which to live."

The original chamber building located on Yuba Street between the Carnegie Library and the railroad tracks.

McDONALD'S CHAPEL/REDDING CEMETERY

Cemeteries were as much a sign of an established community in the developing days of Northern California as were churches and schools. The towns, some never to become incorporated, each sought to develop the communal facilities that made them complete, often relying on religious or fraternal organizations to meet those needs in the absence of formal local government.

In 1879 the 19-acre Redding Cemetery was established on part of the Buenaventura Land Grant at the east end of Eureka Way on the outskirts of the community. It was a joint effort by the Independent Order of Odd Fellows and the Free and Accepted Masons.

Lodge representatives managed the cemetery for nearly 85 years, adding 20 acres in 1903 through the purchase of an adjacent ranch. The governing board became a significant economic force in the community, loaning cemetery funds to area residents, secured by home and business mortgages, and financing cemetery activities with the interest received.

Rudy Balma and his wife, Margaret, in 1955 had acquired from Theodore and Elsie McDonald the McDonald's Chapel in Redding, opened the chapel in Burney in 1958, and in 1960 acquired the chapel in Anderson. Balma had begun working for the McDonalds in 1943 while in high school, left to attend the San Francisco College of Mortuary Science, and returned after college.

By 1964 the chores of cemetery operations had become excessive for the lodges and both fraternities needed funds to renovate or relocate their lodges. The Balmas purchased the Redding Cemetery and have operated it since. A continuing tree-planting program has resulted in a unique collection of nearly every evergreen that can grow in this cli-

McDonald's Chapel, built in 1966, is located on a gentle hillside south of the entrance to the Redding Cemetery.

mate, shading the gentle slopes of the cemetery.

In 1985 the Balmas acquired the Lawncrest Chapel and Memorial Park. They also operate the Burney Cemetery under a management contract with the cemetery district there. Their son, Brian, is a member of the family corporation that operates the chapels and cemeteries.

With the chapel, built in 1966 and located adjacent to the cemetery, the facilities provide mortuary, cemetery, mausoleum, columbarium, and crematory services and facilities all at one location. A Widowhood Outreach Program initiated in 1984 provides programs and support not only for patrons of McDonald's and Lawncrest but for others referred by hospices or the Golden Umbrella.

Balma says that at the present rate of use, the cemetery has adequate space to serve the community for another 75 to 120 years. An irrevocable trust fund has been established using a portion of lot fees, and interest from the trust fund is committed to perpetual maintenance

The imposing gateway to the Redding Cemetery, at the east end of Eureka Way, was installed about 1900 by Elizabeth Litsch Etter "to the memory of her father and mother, Frank and Caroline Litsch, and her friends resting here."

and upkeep of the cemetery.

Balma recently retired from the board of trustees of Mercy Medical Center after services of more than 25 years. He was president of the Shasta Union High School District board during his 16-year tenure on that board, is past president of Redding Rotary Club, and past exalted ruler of the Redding Elks Lodge. He is chairman of the board and an organizing director of the North Valley Bank and is still a member of its board.

PRIVATE INDUSTRY COUNCIL OF SHASTA COUNTY

The Private Industry Council of Shasta County began in 1978 as a mere advisory group to a manpower planning board under the Comprehensive Employment and Training Act (CETA). Today PIC is an independent, nonprofit agency directed by a board of 17 representatives of local business, labor, government agencies, and educators that has become a vital cog in the development of the Shasta County economy.

In just one year (1985) PIC worked with over 1,500 job seekers and placed more than 500 in the local labor market. It operated training activities for electronic circuit board production, clerical, automotive, medical, and service occupations, entered into 364 on-the-job training agreements with local employers, operated a direct placement program in cooperation with the state Employment Development Department, and established a Displaced Worker Center to provide services to nearly 1,000 local workers affected by business closures and reductions.

In eary 1985 PIC also opened an office in Burney to expand services to both unemployed workers and to businesses in the intermountain area.

Operating within the constraints of federal and state legislation, PIC has tailored its program to local circumstances, with emphasis on broad-based economic development, placing local citizens in jobs within the community, providing employment services for local businesses, and training programs for youth, dislocated workers, older job seekers, and others who are earnestly seeking work but lack essential skills to qualify for available openings.

"Performance standards (of PIC) are based on persons obtaining employment and our effectiveness in keeping placement costs low. The council places a premium on employment opportunities in the private sector," says Don Peery, PIC executive director. "The programs are designed to be responsive to the needs of local employers and local job

Alan Hill (left), 1986 chairman of the Private Industry Council of Shasta County, and Donald Peery, executive director, oversee the program designed to bring together local employers and qualified prospective employees.

seekers. PIC also has a history of supporting local job creation through economic development."

Under the past chairmanship of Don Gallino, a local contractor, and currently Alan Hill, PIC developed a two-pronged program. First emphasis is the creation of local jobs through economic development. The second is to place the maximum number of local citizens in new and existing jobs, avoiding the importation of labor into an already job-poor economy.

PIC has funded, through grants, a major part of an industrial outreach program of the Shasta County Economic Development Corporation. Once an interest in Shasta County as an industrial site is developed, the EDC then assists in developing financing and other elements essential to a new plant location. PIC's

Beth Rogers (left) and two trainees are using new vocational testing equipment acquired by the Private Industry Council of Shasta County to help direct applicants into appropriate vocations.

staff helps find local unemployed or underemployed citizens and trains them in the needed skills.

Perhaps the most ambitious undertaking of PIC to date is its creation of the Shasta County Economic Development Task Force. The task force began in 1985 as an ad hoc committee of PIC and, taking on an identity all its own, became a community partnerhsip in the true sense.

Bringing together representatives from business and governmental agencies involved in the development process, and others, the task force established eight subcommittees composed of over 200 county residents to explore the many issues affecting business development and to make recommendations for improvement. The final report included recommendations for action by the many diverse entities involved in business development for the community.

The core of PIC's program, however, is placing local job seekers in the local labor market, and it receives the prime attention of three-fourths of the PIC staff effort. Through the discreet application of grant funds provided under the federal Jobs Training Partnership Act, PIC goes far beyond the traditional referral service of many government agencies.

Worker placement evolves through a wide range of employment and training activities, including pre-employment screening and referrals to the employer's specifications while retaining for the employer all final decisions on hiring; testing, on a customized basis, of potential employees; training programs to meet

specific industry or employer needs; young-adult programs, providing a short initial period of employment at no cost to the employer and tax credits for those ultimately selected; the TEAM program (Targeting Experience and Maturity), which in its first year was contacted by 97 persons over 55 years of age and provided vocational testing, motivational workshops, job-search workshops, and individual placement and on-the-job training interviews; and in-school and summer youth programs, which provided 330 youths with work experience before high school graduation with the Jobs Training Partnership Act funds paying their salaries. Another program reimburses employers for the first 20 hours of wages earned by the youth, who are then eligible to enter the on-the-job training program.

"Our success is measured by our achievement of seven performance goals," Peery explains. "In the 1984-

1985 program year, we exceeded our goals in six of the seven categories and improved over the previous year when we achieved five of the goals. Meeting our performance standards resulted in additional funds through the State's Incentive Award System, which enabled the council to further enhance its program activities and services to Shasta County."

The PIC program is funded with federal grants under Public Law 97300, but a development plan adopted by the PIC board calls for the program to become less dependent on federal funds over the next five years with increasing reliance on public and private grants and service fees.

In summary, the PIC program is designed to reduce the employers' high cost associated with hiring and training new employees, while at the same time assisting motivated local employees to qualify for the work that is available.

REDDING MEDICAL CENTER

The wild, raw, and boisterous town that was Redding for the first half of its 100-year existence has given way to a settled, stable, and pleasant community and has developed into an economic and medical service hub for people living 150 miles in any direction. This evolution of Redding was paralleled by the development of what is now Redding Medical Center, a complete medical facility, an innovator in treatment and facility design, and a hospital capable of providing almost all essential services to the community that has watched and helped it to grow.

In 1908 Dr. Chester J. Teass, company surgeon for the Mammouth Mine in Kennett, treated a constable for a gunshot wound in the chest at the scene of the shooting, and the patient was later moved to the company hospital. Although Teass' prognosis was gloomy, the constable regained consciousness and his complaints prompted Teass to reopen the patient whereupon he found a bullet lodged "in the area of the heart." Teass performed what has been called the first open-heart surgery in history and the constable recovered, bringing a degree of fame to Teass if not to the patient. With the completion of the 1985-1986 addition to Redding Medical Center, Shasta County will have complete modern facilities for open-heart surgery and postoperative recovery unimagined here only 15 years ago, let alone in Teass' era.

In the midst of World War II,

Redding's 10,000 population had only 10 general practitioners when Dr. Thomas Daniel Wyatt, a local physician and graduate of the University of Oregon Medical School, built the original Memorial Hospital of Redding, now known as Redding Medical Center. (It is not clear today to whom it was to be a memorial—Wyatt later told an associate, "It just sounded like a good name" for a hospital.)

Scrounging scarce medical and construction equipment from an abandoned hospital near Shasta Dam and the Mt. Shasta City hospital, Wyatt's hospital opened on May 14, 1945, as a 44-bed general care facility with 30 employees. He later purchased a Redding maternity home and moved that equipment into Memorial.

In January 1954, 10 physicians, a

A pharmacy occupied the Butte and East streets corner of Memorial Hospital of Redding during the early 1960s.

The architect's rendering of Redding Medical Center shows the facility looking east across East Street. The blocks to the left, rear, and right also house community medical facilities or parking space for the hospital.

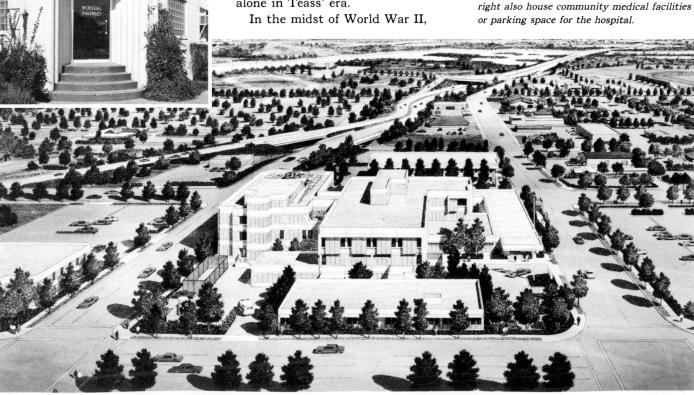

local attorney, and Memorial administrator Robert R. Roberts purchased the facility from Wyatt. Roberts continued as administrator until his retirement in 1972.

Three additions between 1958 and 1963 expanded Memorial's size to 132 beds, and in 1972 it was purchased by National Medical Enterprises, a U.S. firm that has since become the world's second-largest health care services company. A three-story addition was built four years later, updating a 73-patient bed area and adding intensive care, coronary care, and new surgery, laboratory, and X-ray facilities.

In 1982 the hospital saw the creation of what administrator Gerald E. Knepp characterizes as a "superb intensive care unit where the nurses

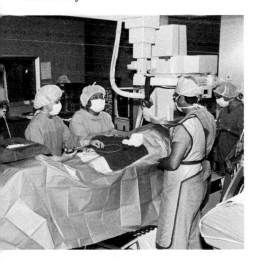

Heart catheterization was an early diagnostic tool at Redding Medical Center. The hospital has now developed into a full-service heart care facility.

are able to stay with the patients continually," and which is being copied at a $100-million hospital currently being built for the University of Southern California by NME.

The hospital's system of maintaining critical patients' charts has been adapted by Stanford University Medical School and others, and a critical care nurses' education pro-

The intensive care unit of Redding Medical Center provides nurse stations in close proximity to all patients.

gram, developed on videotape by Memorial, has been purchased by the University of California-Davis Medical Center and other hospitals for training.

Wellness clinics and health promotion programs, detoxification and chemical dependency treatment, discharge planning and social service, and physical and occupational therapy all have been added as public awareness of the value of preventive and post-treatment care has grown.

Just short of its 40th anniversary, the hospital embarked on the latest of its expansion programs. At a cost of $12.5 million, the project, completed in late 1986, increased the bed capacity from 132 to 190 and added 46,000 square feet of new construction. The name of the facility became Redding Medical Center with the announcement of the expansion-renovation in October 1984.

The privately owned taxpaying medical facility has grown since 1945 from the original 44 beds with 10 general practice physicians available to its present 140,000 square feet of space with 190 beds, six surgery suites, full cardiac treatment facilities, wellness and rehabilitation programs, mobile intensive care ambulance service, and a history of innovative treatment. The medical staff has grown to more than 200, including 22 different specialties. The hospital, which began with 30

employees, now has 400.

Cardiac care has become a major focus of the facility. In 1976 diagnostic heart catheterization was begun here to initiate efforts to provide total heart care. A cardiac rehabilitation program of education and therapy after surgery was begun in 1981. In anticipation of the completion of the new, larger surgical suites in the most recent expansion, Redding Medical Center personnel in 1985 began training in Sacramento with cardiac surgeons who planned to move to Redding after completion of the new facilities. With the operating room personnel trained to work as a team, open-heart surgery began here upon completion of the new construction.

The community plays an active role in the hospital through Redding Medical Center Memorial Foundation, a nonprofit group that raises money for such things as college scholarships for students embarking on health and medical careers, and the hospital auxiliary, a group of men and women who volunteer many hours, providing valuable and much-needed services in almost all areas of the hospital. An 11-member governing board of local business professionals and physicians oversees hospital operations.

The excellence of Redding Medical Center is reflected in the care, compassion, and know-how of everyone from the physician, administrator, and nursing staff to the dietary worker, housekeeper, and community volunteer.

C.M. DICKER, INC.

Dicker's, the department store that Irish immigrant C.M. "Charlie" Dicker founded in 1944, has gone through expansions that at times included stores in San Diego County, Palm Springs, Salinas, Mt. Shasta, and Anderson, California, but the heart and flagship of the C.M. Dicker, Inc., operations has moved only a few hundred feet from its origin in downtown Redding.

Dicker was born in Navan, County Meath, Ireland, on January 19, 1903. He and his parents moved to Saskatoon, Saskatchewan, Canada, in 1910. In 1928 he went to Oakland to work for the H.C. Capwell Co. drygoods store, and Charlie became an American citizen in 1940.

Dicker was a buyer for Capwell's in 1944 when he purchased Casey's department store in Redding with 60 feet of frontage on Market Street, a few doors south of the intersection with Yuba Street. "It was a narrow little 'junior department store' with tiny suitcases on the top shelf for sale, a basement, and a small mezzanine," recalls Boyd Alvord, who was hired in 1950 as an accountant and is now vice-president and chief financial officer. "Mrs. Casey used to save her adding machine tapes, then run them through the machine again on the back side to save money."

Charlie moved to Redding and plunged into an aggressive program to develop his business and assume a leadership role in the community. The store expanded by purchasing adjacent businesses and "knocking down the walls in between," Alvord says, until it had a corner location. Ultimately Dicker moved diagonally across the intersection to the present site.

With the end of World War II, Dicker's sons, Robert, Herbert, and Douglas, returned from the Air Corps, Army, and Marine Corps, respectively, to join their father in the

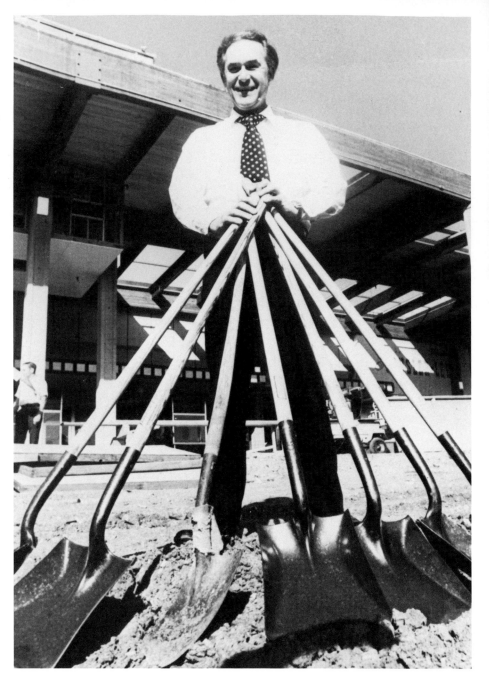

firm, and C.M. devoted increasing attention to activities in support of the community that was supporting his business.

He was chairman of the Greater Redding Chamber of Commerce committee that successfully sought development of Mercy Hospital in Redding. He was instrumental in implementing the Trinity River Project, a multimillion-dollar program that dammed the upper reaches of the Trinity River to divert water into what is now Whiskeytown Lake and ultimately the Sacramento River.

Redding's present city manager form of government is, in part, due to the efforts of C.M. Dicker. Other

The busiest street in Redding was torn up for three blocks and roofed over into an enclosed mall. Robert Dicker led the efforts for the mall construction and participated in the groundbreaking for the Dicker's store with an armload of shovels.

accomplishments included serving as president of the chamber of commerce, as a director of the Redding Rotary Club, a charter member of the Riverview County Club, and a leader in establishing the Salvation Army facility in Redding.

The Irish immigrant son of a onetime colonel in the Fifth Leinster Regiment of the British Army was the first "top hand" in the Redding Asphalt Cowboys.

Irish immigrant C.M. "Charlie" Dicker founded the retail store that bears his name and provides the cornerstone of the Downtown Redding Mall.

In the late 1960s Alvord and Dicker's sons, Robert "Bob" and Herbert, began to purchase the business from C.M., who remained as general manager until his retirement in 1971 and as chairman of the board until his death in 1978. When Bob took over active management of the firm in 1971, he had already followed his father into a community leadership role.

He had spearheaded efforts culminating in creation of the Downtown Redding Mall, one of the first air-conditioned malls in the nation. Through a combination of federal, local, and private financing, three blocks of Market Street and the frontage buildings were enclosed and rebuilt. Air conditioning, interior landscaping and decorating, and renovation or remodeling of most buildings contributed to the establishment in 1972 of the only enclosed shopping mall north of Sacramento and south of Medford, Oregon.

Prior to and after completion of the mall, the Dicker organization purchased many of the buildings making up the complex and sought businesss that would complement each other and stimulate foot traffic into the area.

In 1975 the firm purchased a controlling interest in the Walker Scott Co., a 14-store chain in San Diego County, and operated it until 1985 when those outlets were sold. Other ventures included outlets in Salinas, Mt. Shasta City, and Anderson, California.

Today's Dicker's, which began with about 20,000 square feet of floor space and 20 employees, now occupies 60,000 square feet with up to 60 employees. With the exception of yard goods, the store is still sell-ing the same basic line of ready-to-wear clothing, costume jewelry, personal items, and light appliances that C.M. Dicker established soon after his first acquisition.

During the development of the mall project, Bob Dicker correctly forecast the shift of much of the retail center of Redding from downtown to the east across the Sacramento River. He felt the mall development, coupled with the nearby government buildings and private offices, would provide stability and avoid the core city blight that struck so many areas in the 1960s and 1970s as freeway construction altered the patterns of the community.

He also was instrumental in the development of the Downtown Redding Business Association, designed to promote the entire downtown

Dicker's began as a narrow-front department store that ultimately expanded, during the 1950s, to this location at the corner of Butte and Market streets in downtown Redding.

area. "This area has a character, a personality, and a history, and we believe in it," says Tim Dicker, Bob's son, store buyer, and the third generation involved in the firm's management.

"Our management always took a highly visible and active role in the community," Alvord says. "It was a major factor in our success."

MERCY MEDICAL CENTER

While Mercy Medical Center Redding had its formal beginning in 1944, the evolution of this outstanding medical facility actually began on September 21, 1907, when Dr. Ferdinand Stabel opened St. Caroline Hospital at the corner of Pine and Sacramento streets.

A converted residence, Stabel's $30,000 facility was damaged by fire the next year, and a second fire in 1909 destroyed the hospital.

The St. Caroline Sanitarium was

On July 12, 1951, Redding Mayor Wilber D. Simons sat at the controls of an earth mover in groundbreaking ceremonies for Mercy Hospital. Other participants in the program included (left to right) C.M. Dicker, Fred Smith, Sister Mary Joseph, Sister Elizabeth, and Bristol Hood.

The impressive Mercy Medical Center building perched atop Clairmont Heights has been a highly visible landmark in Redding for more than 30 years. It is now undergoing expansion and modernization to increase services to the community.

built on the site a year later by Stabel and operated until 1944, when a $10,000 donation from the City of Redding and $20,000 provided by the Sisters of Mercy purchased the 45-bed St. Caroline, which was renamed Mercy Hospital. The Sisters had provided health care for residents of Northern California since their arrival in Sacramento in 1857, and hospital care since 1895, and their move into Red-

ding was eagerly sought by a community suffering from a shortage of medical services during World War II.

Within three years the Sisters purchased an imposing 11.5-acre site atop Clairmont Heights overlooking the city, and announced plans for a new hospital. The initial proposal called for a $300,000 facility, but when it was dedicated in 1953 the project had grown to $1.8 million and provided 113 needed beds for the community.

Ten years later a $315,000 pediatric pavilion was dedicated, and in 1968 a $1.4-million expansion program led to the opening of the east wing, increased bed space to 164,

and provided a cardiac care unit, additional obstetrics facilities, a pharmacy, and improved central and cafeteria services.

Only five years later ground was broken for a $6.5-million project that included the addition of 84,000 square feet, demolition and replacement of the administrative wing, expansion of the emergency care center, and modern equipment for a cancer treatment center. That project was completed on February 22, 1975, and in August the name was changed to Mercy Medical Center to reflect more fully the expanded services.

A $30-million construction project begun in 1985 will provide an expanded (44-bed) oncology department, a remodeled pediatrics section, a major increase in the clinical laboratory, a new cardiac care unit, a free-standing radiation oncology building, a remodeled obstetrics unit, improved kitchen and cafeteria, renovation of the main nursing floor, and additional parking spaces to accommodate more than 000 full-

and part-time employees, a medical staff of more than 220, vendors, and visitors.

In 1985 the Clairmont Medical Building near the hospital was purchased and converted into the 5,800-square-foot Mercy outpatient surgical center. The outpatient facility now sends patients home the same day after treatment that formerly required several days of hospitalization.

In the early 1960s the Sisters

An expanded oncology department at Mercy Medical Center is a key element of the $30-million expansion program begun in 1985.

Obstetrics and pediatric care have long been major concerns of the medical center.

knew that the hospital and its area were growing so quickly that a formalized link to the community was necessary. That year the Mercy Advisory Board was formed, and it continues to this day as a vital liaison between the medical center and the community and an important counseling group to the Mercy staff. By 1969, however, it became apparent that Mercy needed even more authoritative direction from its community, business, and civic leaders to respond to growing local needs and the new Medicare regulations.

Mercy's first directors, now trustees, were chairman A.D. Wilkinson, Rudy V. Balma, Dr. Vonnie Dunston, administrator Robert F. Stephenson, and Sister Eileen Barrett, Sister M. Celestine Dyer, and Sister M. St. John Hall. Balma assumed the chairmanship in 1971 after Wilkinson's death and served until 1975 and again from 1982 to 1983. He retired from the board in 1985.

Mercy's growth is more than cement, glass, wiring, and plumbing. Throughout the 40 years of growing pains, the hospital has been quick to respond to a wide range of community needs. "Many of our programs are people-to-people oriented, and not bricks and mortar services of the past. Health care is in an era of dramatic and positive changes which will keep people well and reduce costs. . . . (Our) programs are designed to keep people healthy or keep them out of the hospital, and have lowered Mercy's inpatient activity over the past few years, but we feel that means we are doing our job—making people well faster," George A. Govier, chief executive officer, says.

Among the ancillary programs offered at Mercy are:

Air Ambulance—Two twin-engine aircraft and a helicopter bring patients from remote areas to the central facility or ferry patients to other hospitals for specialized treatment.

Lifeline—The Lifeline program provides, through community dona-

tions, equipment that elderly and/or handicapped people living alone can wear and which, when activated, automatically alerts the hospital through regular telephone circuits that something may be amiss.

Homecare—A 15-person staff of registered nurses, home health aides, physical, speech, and occupational therapists, and social workers makes nearly 800 home visits each month to patients needing skilled care but not requiring hospitalization. The program keeps the patient in the home environment, the staff provides a trained link to the hospital, and costs are drastically reduced over inpatient hospital care.

Hospice Program—A staff of professionals and 56 trained volunteers assists patients and family members to cope with life-threatening illness through counseling, in-home assistance, group meetings and classes, and other means.

Senior Nutrition Program—Sponsored by Mercy and subsidized by state and federal grants, the program provides more than 14,000 hot meals to senior citizens each month, and also transports citizens to and from hot lunch programs and to critical medical services.

Healthline—This program seeks to improve life habits including weight control, smoking cessation, physical fitness, and stress management.

Classes—Classes at Mercy for the public include CPR, diabetic training, prepared childbirth, Alzheimer's disease support group, pediatrics, natural family planning, and prenatal care.

LIVINGSTON INDUSTRIES, INC.

When Shasta County governments and local citizens pooled their resources in 1968 to create the Mountain Lake Industrial Park, Livingston Industries, Inc., did not exist. Yet today it sits quietly on Caterpillar Lane, almost the epitome of the type of industry that most modern communities hope to attract to strengthen their economic base.

Russ Livingston, founder, majority stockholder, president, and chief executive of the corporation that bears his name, oversees a still-expanding business that grew from 50 employees its first year in Shasta County (1975) to the current 125 and in 1986 plans to expand its building from 23,000 to 43,000 square feet of floor space.

The firm is a major subcontractor for the Air Force and several private aircraft jet engine manufacturers, primarily supplying "shielded components," or electrical devices designed to prevent the electrical impulses of an engine from disturbing on-board electronic equipment or providing a "signal" that could be detected by search or homing devices.

Russ Livingston and Maxene Berry packaging military ignition units for shipment.

Russ Livingston and Dorothy Smith providing a final inspection of aircraft engine ignition cables.

Born in Toronto, Canada, on February 8, 1921, Livingston moved with his parents to California six years later. An honor roll student, he dropped out of high school to work during the Depression years, but returned to graduate in 1940. In 1942 he enlisted in the Army, where testing revealed an extremely high aptitude for mechanics. He was enrolled in a crash course in electrical engineering and later received instruction in automatic artillery controls and equipment.

After the war Livingston returned to Southern California and a draftsman's job at Hallett Manufacturing Co., where he had worked briefly before enlisting. After five years and several promotions, he rose to the position of engineering manager, then shifted to the sales department which he ultimately managed. He then became production manager, western division manager, and in 1970 vice-president and general manager. That year Hallett, founded in 1916, declared voluntary bankruptcy and Livingston was asked by bank creditors to reorganize the firm.

With two partners, Robert Wilson and Robert Rutter, Livingston and his wife, Bee, decided to refinance the business. They sold their home, cashed in insurance policies and other assets, and Livingston Industries was born. Rutter is now vice-president and plant manager, and Wilson is vice-president in charge of purchasing and bidding.

In 1975 officers of the still-struggling firm looked for a new location and flew as far north in California as possible—Redding—with the intention of looking at all the communities between there and Los Angeles.

Redding's newly created industrial park, which Livingston describes as having a "good, reliable work force," and the surrounding recreation areas convinced the partners to look no farther. Livingston Industries moved to Redding that

Metal braiding of ignition cable by Linda Koenen.

year, bringing six employees with it and hiring and training the balance locally to produce the parts so critical to military engines.

When high-voltage electrical charges are intermittently sent through a spark plug cable or other electrical transmission line, an electromagnetic field is created that may cause interference or static in other nearby electric or electronic equipment.

While the disturbance can be a nuisance in an automobile radio, it can be downright devastating in a high-performance jet aircraft dependent upon thousands of sophisticated navigation, fire control, communications, or other devices. By providing a shield—usually metallic—around the transmission wire and other components of the ignition system, electrical interference can be eliminated.

Livingston Industries annually uses tons of stainless steel, brass, copper, special alloys, and plastic and fiber insulating material to produce millions of shielded ignition components for general aviation, the Air Force and Army, and the automotive and boating industries.

Although the process varies with the product, a simple spark plug wire may begin as a length of insulated wire fed through a machine that braids as many as 12 fine wires in a tight pattern around the insulation. The steel wire provides a shield surrounding the transmission wire, and blocks the escape of electrical interference into nearby space. The shielded wire is then cut to length, fittings are placed on each end, and it is ready for testing and shipment.

Other units may be encased in a flexible metal tubing, formed around the wire by a machine that in one operation interlocks strips of metal, inserts a fine solder wire, and heats the unit to melt the solder. Another process provides not only an electri-

---

The Livingston Industries, Inc., plant on Caterpillar Lane in the Mountain Lake Industrial Park, Redding.

cal shield but a rigid watertight housing as well.

While Livingston Industries possesses the skills and equipment to manufacture nearly all parts used in its assembly process, many of the precision fittings are farmed out to machine shops organized for that specific type of production.

Generally, the work day starts at 5 a.m., but employees can change their hours to serve their needs and leave during the day if necessary, returning to finish their shift. "We started here 11 years ago, and 20 percent of our employees have been with us 10 years or more," Livingston says. Most of the work is not done on an assembly line, but rather with an employee working through several boxes of unfinished products, perhaps soldering several connections on each, or attaching fittings, or testing the completed product.

Livingston products have twice won awards from the Defense Department for quality and excellence, and the firm is the only contractor to win consecutive awards. Most aircraft parts production is coded so that a defective part, if found, can be traced back to the original manufacturer. Aircraft engine manufacturers supplied by Livingston include Pratt & Whitney, Garrett Corporation, Lycoming, and Solar of San Diego.

SHASTA SISKIYOU TRANSPORT

Shasta Siskiyou Transport and its predecessor firms share a 100-year history with Redding, beginning with bricks and ending with a tanker fleet.

Redding's development in the first 100 years evolved around two major factors:

Geographically, it is in a keystone position at the north end of the Sacramento-San Joaquin Valley where the Coast Range and the Cascades funnel transportation on the nation's major Pacific Coast highway through a narrow corridor crossed by the first major east-west highway north of Sacramento. Today, as in the later half of the nineteenth century, nearly all landbound commerce for a vast area larger than many states must pass through or near Redding.

Abundant natural resources— gold, copper, water, and timber— provided well-paying work for those willing to labor in the mines, forests, and heavy-construction industries.

In the late 1880s, shortly after the railroad entered Shasta County, the Holt and Gregg Co. moved its brick factory from Red Bluff to

In 1887 this was the Holt and Gregg Co. Brick Manufacturing plant. Located between Redding and Anderson, the 160-acre site was later occupied by the US Plywood/ Champion mill complex.

Shasta County and created a new brick factory, kilns, and clay pit on the 160-acre site that decades later would become the US Plywood-Champion mill in Anderson.

Because of inadequate fire protection, bricks were still the preferred construction material, and for the next 30 years Holt and Gregg provided most of the bricks used in Northern California and constructed most of the old brick buildings— many still standing—from southern Oregon through the upper Sacramento Valley.

In 1891 James R. Holt moved his family into a fine brick home at the corner of Butte and West streets in Redding, which is still in use today and houses a local law firm. The old Shasta County High School and many other old county buildings were constructed of Holt and Gregg bricks: McCormick & Saeltzer Co. (1888), the Golden Eagle Hotel (1896), the Lorenz Hotel (1902), and the Redding City Hall (1906).

Holt and his partner, John Gregg, also developed a limestone quarry at Kennett, selling to the local copper smelters the flux needed to refine the copper ore. The quarry also

provided the lime for the mortar used in laying up the millions of bricks coming out of the factory at Anderson.

James R. Holt died in 1913 and was succeeded in the company by his son, James Chesley Holt. Holt and Gregg closed the Redding Brick Yard and sold the Kennett Limestone Quarry in 1921 to U.S. Smelting and Refining Co. The smelters had closed and construction had declined. Shasta County's population in 1910 was 19,000, but by 1920 it was down to 13,000.

Redding's first service station appeared in 1920, and the next year James Holt and Milton Heryford established a Cadillac, Chevrolet, and White agency on California Street. The agency was sold in 1926 and Holt began work at Vern Ferguson's Mobil Station and soon was offered a sales representative job with General Petroleum (Mobil).

In 1928 the Texas Company (Texaco) built a bulk plant at Old Highway 99 and Wyndham Lane in Redding. Holt bought a 385-gallon tank truck and became Texas Company's commission agent for Shasta and Trinity counties. Through the

A new White truck sold by the Heryford and Holt Cadillac, Chevrolet, and White Agency in Redding is climbing the Round Mountain Grade about 1921. James C. Holt is beside the car.

Depression he kept the business going with deliveries to gold dredges, family sawmills, and a few low-volume service stations.

Between 1938 and 1940 Redding's population doubled as construction began on Shasta Dam. Business soared until 1942, when World War II gasoline rationing pushed sales back down to the Depression-era levels.

The General Petroleum Bulk Plant (Mobil) at Chico in 1926. Sales representative Jim Holt is by the car on the far left.

The early postwar years saw an exodus of construction workers after completion of Shasta Dam and an influx of wood workers as demand for home building materials increased. Holt died in 1949, but the Texas Company management had held him in such high regard that it allowed his 22-year-old son, James Cravens Holt, to become the commission agent at the firm's Redding plant.

Redding was entering a 25-year boom. International corporations were building huge wood-products plants, major highways and dams were being constructed, and recreational resorts and marinas were springing up to accommodate tourists and business travelers. "We were selling to wholesalers, retailers, to the mills, the construction industry, and the loggers. Jobs were plen-

tiful, wages were high, the saloons were full, and the area prospered," Holt recalls.

In the 1960s the men who had built Texaco had been replaced by a new generation. The Texas Company became Texaco Inc., the headquarters was moved from Houston to New York City, and new sales policies were initiated. In 1967 Holt terminated his contract with Texaco

and moved his firm into the Phillips 66 plant at Redding. In 1967 a court decision on an antitrust case forced Phillips 66 out of the West Coast market and SST became an unbranded marketer.

Mobil Oil Corporation by 1978 was closing distributor plants throughout much of Northern California and planned to close its plant in Redding. SST needed a major brand, so it bought the commission distributorship and operated the

plant at a loss until 1980 when it purchased the plant.

Under the administration of Jim Holt, president; Bob Gray, vice-president/marketing; and Paul Wellington, vice-president/operations, along with the cooperation of a fine team of highly qualified employees, SST has become the leading petroleum marketer in the 12 Northern California and Oregon counties it serves and is among the 50 highest-volume Mobil Oil distributors in the United States.

A 1986 photo of some of Shasta Siskiyou Transport's 32 tank trucks and tank trailers between shifts at the Redding yard.

Holt's 385-gallon tank truck at the Texaco Bulk Plant at Highway 99 South and Wyndham Lane in Redding in 1928.

SST has 45 employees in Redding with an annual payroll of more than one million dollars and pays over $10 million in federal, state, county, and city taxes per year. Its environmental and safety programs have resulted in a near-perfect record of no explosions, fires, or major spills of hazardous or toxic materials.

COUNTRY NATIONAL BANK

On March 11, 1985, Country National Bank of Redding opened its doors for the first time to the public and customers, offering a personal physical atmosphere and a wide range of banking services developed by 18 local organizers and developers.

At the end of the first calendar year, M.R. Tandy, Country National executive vice-president, announced total assets of more than $14 million on hand and a bright future for the bank, which offers a wide range of services to both individuals and small to medium-size businesses. Tandy says that more than 2,000 customers had been attracted to the bank in less than 10 months of operation, with significant activity in the real estate market.

With its emphasis on personal service between banker and customer

be found in a more stereotyped concrete, steel, and tile facility.

The concept of Country National began in 1983, when Tandy, who had over 17 years' experience in finance and banking in the Redding area, and others felt that the community was ready for a new, locally owned, and independent federal bank. After research of the

Two and one-half million dollars in stock was sold for organizing capital, and construction of the American traditional-style building on

Country National Bank welcomed its first customers on March 11, 1985, to this location on Hilltop Drive.

and direct access to the decision makers, the bank has developed a significant portion of its business among the professionals and small-business people of the community. The interior design of the bank, with a fireplace lounge area, open-beam ceilings, and unobstructed view of all activities, contributes to the "country" ambiance and reduces the feeling of intimidation that might

The interior decor of the bank is designed to provide warmth, comfort, and easy accessibility to the bank personnel.

community and existing services and development of a marketing plan, ultimately 18 community residents and leaders were involved in an application to the Comptroller of the Currency for a charter.

Hilltop Drive was undertaken in 1984.

Officers of the bank are R.D. "Dan" Gover, Cottonwood rancher and former county supervisor, school board chairman, and active participant in many community and agricultural organizations, chairman of the board; William M. Reus III, D.D.S., secretary; Anna B. Riley, with over 32 years of banking experience, including 22 years in the Redding area, vice-president and chief financial officer; and Tandy, executive vice-president and senior loan officer.

Other directors include David P. Bruck, Donald Dawson, Philip J. Grauel, Richard C. Guiton, Eugene L. Ireland, M.D., Randall P. Lush, Jerry D. McDonald, Sim Nathan, Robert K. Peterson, Roy W. Ramsey, Charles J. Raudman, Richard S. Steffens, Jr., M.D., and Raymond E. Toney.

NICHOLS, MELBURG, AND ROSSETTO, A.I.A.

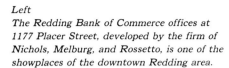

Left
The Redding Bank of Commerce offices at 1177 Placer Street, developed by the firm of Nichols, Melburg, and Rossetto, is one of the showplaces of the downtown Redding area.

Above
When the City of Redding constructed the Convention and Visitors' Bureau offices on Auditorium Drive in 1985, it turned to Nichols, Melburg, and Rossetto for the architectural design.

The architectural firm of Nichols, Melburg, and Rossetto has been involved in projects large and small throughout Northern California, applying the skills and training of the three partners and a staff of 11 others to develop a project from concept through design and construction to completion.

Eugene Nichols, the managing partner, came to Redding in 1966 and became a partner in a local firm, which has evolved through the years into Nichols, Melburg, and Rossetto, with the association of Les Melburg and Dan Rossetto. All three are registered architects and members of the American Institute of Architects.

The senior partner has had responsibility for the Siskiyou County Jail project, the Chico Pacific Telephone and Telegraph Building, church buildings for the Church of Jesus Christ of Latter Day Saints throughout Northern California, the award-winning Redding Bank of Commerce, medical buildings in Redding, and Bank of America institutions in Redding, Red Bluff, and other Northern California sites.

Melburg, who is the partner in charge of design and planning, joined the firm in 1975—with intermittent

time off to complete his requirements for a degree in architecture from California Polytechnic State University in 1981. He has won several design awards, including an honor award for the Shasta Enterprises office building and a merit award presented by the Masonry Institute for his endeavor on the Redding Bank of Commerce. He made a presentation of the firm's accomplishments at the Monterey Design Conference sponsored by the American Institute of Architects, and several of his projects have been published in trade and architecture magazines.

Rossetto received his bachelor of architecture degree from California Polytechnic State University in 1973, and has a comprehensive background in large corporate and public works projects. His clients have included the U.S. Navy, Pacific Gas and Electric Company, Bank of America, and numerous school districts. He is project architect for the U.S. Postal Service General Mail Facility in Redding.

Right
Architectural firm partners (left to right) Dan Rossetto, Eugene Nichols, and Les Melburg have been involved in a wide range of projects in Shasta County and Northern California.

Right
Nichols, Melburg, and Rossetto was the architect for the Shasta Enterprises office at 400 Redcliff Drive in Redding.

PARACLIPSE, INC.

Each time a shuttle flight is launched from the NASA Kennedy Space Center in Florida, a group of satellite television antennae built in Redding makes a contribution to America's space program.

These antennae are the product of Paraclipse, Inc., a Redding firm that is the world's largest manufacturer of high-performance, high-technology satellite TV antennae only two years after its own launch—truly a space age success story.

NASA's Paraclipse antennae handle a variety of tasks, ranging from monitoring the weather to facilitating network television coverage of space launches. They also are used for training and teleconferencing. And, as they do for hundreds of thousands of home owners, the NASA antennae also provide our astronauts with the wide choice of entertainment that only satellite television can offer.

The first Paraclipse antenna was built in the Redding garage of company founder David Johnson. As a partner in an antenna retail dealership during the industry's fledgling years, Johnson, then 30, felt that the satellite television market would never realize its full potential unless antennae offered performance and durability far superior to any then available.

Because these antennae reach into the vastness of space to pull an extremely weak signal down to earth, and greatly amplify it, their parabolic shape must be highly accurate and symmetrical. Surface variations as small as 3/8 inch would greatly compromise performance.

To secure the level of marketing acceptance Johnson believed possible, the "right" antenna would have to satisfy some very critical performance and manufacturing criteria.

It had to be mass-producible in a

David Johnson, president, shows models of two antennae that made Paraclipse Shasta County's largest industrial employer in only five years. Photo by Mark Fator

way that made it totally dependable, easily shipped and assembled, and, most important of all, absolutely repeatable. It had to go together the same way—work the same way—every time out of the box. And it also had to look a lot better than the big solid dishes that were keeping a lot of buyers out of the market at that time.

After several months of considering and rejecting designs, Johnson was returning from a service call to a customer who lived "way back in the mountains west of Redding" when he hit on a concept that seemed to meet all of his criteria. It called for a heavy-duty expanded aluminum-mesh dish supported by the same interlocking rib and ring truss system that Paraclipse uses today.

On June 1, 1981, Paradigm Manufacturing, Inc., was formed to produce this antenna. With dictionaries

This aluminum and steel satellite television antenna is the product of the nation's largest manufacturer of antennae only a short time after the firm's founding in Redding.

defining "paradigm" as a "pattern, example, model. . .a design worth copying," the corporate name would prove prophetic.

The firm's antennae would revolutionize the satellite television industry, attracting many imitators as they quickly became the standard for performance, reliability, and ease of installation the world over.

The first manufacturing facility on Cascade Boulevard in Central Valley had only 2,000 square feet of floor space, six employees, and a monthly production of 10 units—most of them sold locally.

But beginning in 1983, keyed to the phenomenal growth of the industry it was helping to pioneer, a series of rapid expansions shot the firm past an interim 8,000-square-foot facility on East Side Road to its current six-building, 141,000-square-foot complex on Meadowview Drive next to Redding's Municipal Airport.

In two meteoric years the company achieved the largest production capacity in its industry, international distribution, and the largest work force—about 250—of any locally owned industrial manufacturer.

When the name of its antennae (Paraclipse) became better known than its corporate name (Paradigm), a separate Paraclipse, Inc., organization was formed to market the product, and today both the company and its antennae are known as "Paraclipse."

From its inception the firm has actively participated in the work of its industry's trade groups, with Johnson selected as president and chairman of the Satellite Television Industry Association.

A substantial portion of the Paraclipse marketing effort is educationally oriented—committed to showing the public how satellite television works and providing guidelines for selecting complete systems geared to specific geographic areas and programming interests.

A point of special pride among those who have contributed to the success of Paraclipse is that it was achieved "with no outside help."

"Everything we've accomplished," Johnson confirms, "has been made possible by local people. We didn't bring in experts from out of town. We didn't go to anybody other than local people for anything we did.

"Our general manager, Jack Connelly, was the administrator of Shasta General Hospital. The head of our engineering department, Gene Willyard, started out in the plant with broom or wrench in his hands, whatever was needed.

"People with absolutely no previous experience welding aluminum suddenly found themselves building state-of-the-art satellite antennae. And we purchased all of our materials locally if we possibly could, even our steel. We are basically a local, home-grown, home-owned company.

"This area is also excellent for market testing, because, with one of the earliest and heaviest concentrations of satellite antennae in America, the Redding market historically runs about a year ahead of the rest of the country. So we use it for many of our market test studies.

"When you stop to think about it," Johnson points out, "there is a sort of 'high tech moves north' perspective to our being located here. Every day, NASA—the center of science for our country, the world, really—is applying technology that has its roots in rural America.

"It started here. Now we're building it here, too."

Six buildings provide 141,000 square feet of floor space for the Paraclipse factory, located on Meadowview Drive adjacent to the Redding Municipal Airport.

VOORWOOD COMPANY

Barney Street in Anderson is a somewhat backwater area—a block-long dead end. Once a part of the main north-south arterial in Northern California, it has been twice bypassed by highway improvement projects; and, although visible from elevated I-5 going through Anderson, a casual sightseer would rarely be there.

Yet Voorwood Company, at 2350 Barney Street, is a major player in the world furniture market—and visitors from anywhere in the world may come to the small manufacturing facility to learn to operate the automated equipment they have purchased to manufacture furniture and other specialty wood products.

Ted Voorhees, president of the firm, studied forestry at Oregon State College, but left after three and one-half years to go into the log-hauling business. He then moved to the California north coast as part owner of a planing mill until he decided in 1960 to move to Cottonwood (in southern Shasta County) and open a similar operation there. His partner was his brother, Jerry, with whom he has been associated in business for more than twenty-six years, and who is executive vice-president for Voorwood Company. pany.

After a brief period producing molding, the two men went into machinery manufacture, producing some of the lighter board-handling equipment for sawmills. In the mid-1960s they were approached by Kimberly-Clark Corporation, which was then operating a large sawmill only a few hundred yards from the small Voorhees machine shop. Kimberly-Clark was interested in developing and marketing a molding made from finger-jointed small scraps of pine and fir and covered with a vinyl coating printed to resemble expensive—and scarce—hardwoods.

Ted Voorhees, president of Voorwood Company.

Jerry Voorhees, executive vice-president.

"We made a quotation on the machine, but it took us a year to develop the first one," Ted Voorhees says. "We had a lot of headaches making that first machine work, but now it is almost automatic—just like starting your car."

Just as the vinyl-covered molding proved superior to previous efforts to paint a pattern onto the wood, today newer products, called "foil," have generally replaced vinyl. Voorhees said the process uses an extremely thin and scratch resistant "high pressure" paper, which is temporarily bonded to a clear plastic carrier. Coated with greatly improved adhesives, the material is applied to shaped molding through a combination of heat and rollers positioned to press the grain-patterned paper onto the softwood.

Most of the equipment produced today by Voorwood, is designed to shape wooden pieces to the desired pattern, sand or finish it, apply the printed pattern, and trim off any ex-

cess—all in one operation.

The firm designs and builds most of the components of its sophisticated machinery, often literally starting with only an idea or a need; some blocks of steel, aluminum, and cast iron; a sketch pad; and a graphic-design computer. From those elements a $50,000 to $100,000 machine may be developed.

A complete machine shop in the plant includes equipment for forming, bending, cutting, welding, and shaping metal. Cutting heads to form the wood are shaped from solid steel blocks, then carbide cutting knives are attached by silver solder before being formed on a grinder to the profile desired to cut a specified pattern. Sanding rings, formerly purchased from a German manufacturer, are now produced by Voorwood at the Anderson plant.

The stock, or wood to be covered, may be held in place and fed into the machine by means of a vacuum table or by rollers and pressure devices, depending upon the shape to be developed. All control panels, electrical and mechanical parts, are produced in the 17,000-square-foot shop.

Each machine is designed for a specific type of production—molding for desk edges, door jambs, or window frames; flat laminators to cover veneers or high-density composition board made from wood fibers; picture frames; furniture parts; or bathroom and kitchen cabinets.

One Voorwood machine built for a customer in Thailand gathered jute strings from 360 rolls, glued them to a paper backing, then calendered or pressed the assembled paper and jute into a wallpaper.

"Nearly every unit we build is unique," the company's founder states. "They are customized to fit the needs of the purchaser. We keep designing machines that industry wants, but mostly for furniture and cabinet work. Every machine is operated in our shop before we send it out; we send a comprehensive manual with every machine, and sometimes

I, or Jerry, or one of our technicians will go with a machine overseas to help get it started. But many of the foreign buyers like to send a representative here. It gives them an opportunity for a 'business vacation.'"

The manufacture of furniture, cabinets, and miscellaneous wood products is termed "secondary wood processing" and is a large international industry. Southern California alone employs approximately 35,000 people in this field, primarily in the production of furniture. Nationally, it employs 540,000 people, with 197,000 in furniture making, and sales top $13.4 billion annually.

Voorwood Company, makes a spe-

cial product to meet a very narrow need of that industry, both domestic and foreign. Only two or three firms in the United States and a few elsewhere make machines designed to do the same work as the Voorwood equipment. "The machines are expensive, they last a long time, and production from a single machine is high," president Voorhees said. However, that limited market is providing steady work for a skilled crew of fifty in Shasta County—and shows signs only of growth.

Voorwood Company began at its new site in this corrugated steel shed in 1963.

The work crew is assembled before the new plant, constructed in 1979 to house the machinery manufacturing firm.

NORTHSTAR AVIATION CENTER

Nearly every element of commercial and private aviation except aircraft manufacture and scheduled airline operation is encompassed by Northstar Aviation Center, a growing Redding business that began out of its owner's personal need for business transportation in 1967.

Gerald Griffith was in the survey and engineering business with five offices in California and crews flying around California, Nevada, and Oregon in connection with their work. To facilitate the essential air transportation, Griffith's office was moved to the Redding Skyranch Airport, located south of Redding. When the Redding Skyranch and the fixed-based operations of Shasta Aviation, Inc., were offered for sale in July 1977, Griffith purchased both the airport and the fixed-base operations.

Within two years Griffith needed more space and additional facilities and, as a result, purchased Northstar Aviation. Northstar got its start in 1967 as the first fixed-base operator at the Redding Municipal Airport, under the name of Beva Aero. It was purchased by John Herbert of Redding in 1975, who in turn sold to Griffith. At that time Northstar had 10 employees. As the Northstar Aviation Center operations grew at the municipal airport, Griffith, in 1982, sold the Skyranch property and facilities and also sold his survey and engineering firm to devote his full time to Northstar.

Today Northstar is involved in nearly every phase of general aviation except the manufacture of aircraft. The work force of 10 that Griffith first employed at Northstar has now grown to 60, including

Avionics, the maintenance of aircraft radios and navigational equipment, is part of the full range of services offered by Northstar in Redding.

Overnight freight delivery keeps Northstar planes in the air with 10 different routes in California and Nevada.

maintenance mechanics, pilots, line service employees, and sales and administrative personnel. Northstar operates 24 aircraft, which it either owns or leases on a full-time basis, and has aircraft and crews based in Reno, Sacramento, Oakland, Arcata, Salinas, and Redding.

"Northstar is many businesses rolled into one," says Griffith. "Aircraft maintenance and repair, parts sales, avionics, (sales and service of radios and navigational equipment), engine overhauls, insurance repair work, air freight, charter service, flight instruction, fueling and line service. We do it all."

Although only one aircraft was initially involved in 1981, Northstar today finds itself an important factor in the burgeoning overnight freight and mail business, running

10 different routes daily for United Parcel Service, five days per week, in California and Nevada with occasional special charter flights for other air freighters. Each route is a complete circle with several stops, and the assigned aircraft are modified to handle freight rather than passengers.

In 1984 UPS management honored Northstar Aviation Center by selecting it as the number one UPS carrier in the country. "Their pilots fly under some of the most adverse conditions in the country, encountering fog in the valleys and icing and turbulence over the Sierra Nevada and Coast Range," noted one UPS executive when stating that the award was based on "on-time departures, dependability, mechanical reliability, and all-round service."

The Shasta County banks have discovered that dependability of service, and Northstar now regularly flies bank documents and papers from Redding to the bank clearing houses in the Bay Area to minimize lost time and interest for the banks.

Another regular activity of Northstar Aviation Center gears up each summer as its local pilots overfly the logging areas east of Redding at the end of each work day and after every lightning storm to provide early forest fire detection. According to Griffith, there have been a number of fires that have been spotted and put out without major damage. "After a good lightning storm, there can be hundreds of fires started," he says.

The fires are reported to the California Department of Forestry, the involved timber companies, and to the U.S. Forest Service if they occur on federal lands. Northstar aircraft are sometimes directed to stay at the scene of the fire and provide airborne controller facilities for the government water-drop bombers fly-

ing in to attack the fires.

Although Northstar does not operate any scheduled air passenger routes, the commercial airlines contribute to the flow of out-of-town money that supports the firm. Fueling service, emergency maintenance, and overnight cleaning of aircraft all have been performed by the firm's crew, which also provides backup support for the Department of Forestry and U.S. Forest Service crews stationed at Redding.

Essentially any form of aircraft maintenance is within the skills and capability of Northstar personnel, and they have undertaken several restoration projects on damaged aircraft. In 1984 a large Beechcraft Super Kingair was damaged in a landing near La Paz, Mexico. The

company ferried the plane to Redding, then undertook complete rebuilding of engine and frame.

Insurance repair is a significant portion of the firm's work and is augmented by private aircraft from all over Northern California, southern Oregon, and eastern Nevada, which are flown to Redding for Northstar maintenance of engines and avionics.

Northstar Aviation Center is a dealer for Cessna aircraft and an authorized service center for Cessna, Piper, and Mooney.

Engine and airframe repair and maintenance are conducted by Northstar mechanics on a wide range of aircraft brought to the firm's Redding facility.

RECORD SEARCHLIGHT

To nearly 100,000 readers who turn to it daily except Sunday, the *Record Searchlight* is a source of the latest in news, commentary, features, and advertising about their community, region, and the world.

The newspaper will celebrate its 50th birthday in 1988, but its ancestral roots extend back to the Gold Rush days. The *Shasta Courier*, founded in 1850, was the area's first newspaper, and its name continues today in the *Record Searchlight's* masthead.

When the *Redding Record* debuted in the fall of 1938, it did so in competition with two morning newspapers—the *Independent* and the *Searchlight*—and with the *Courier-Free Press* in the afternoon. Additionally, the outspoken *Shasta Dial* was published once a week.

The *Record* was founded by editor Paul C. Bodenhamer and business manager Harry O. Bostwick as a member of the John P. Scripps Newspaper Group. Bodenhamer and Bostwick were employed by Scripps newspapers in the Ventura area and were asked by company officials to explore the possibilities of founding a new newspaper in Redding. They arrived on a scorching July day. Bodenhamer was to recall later that "there were more bars than churches. The red-light district was extensive and obvious, and half-dollars were the medium of exchange."

The *Record* was started on a shoestring, with a minimum of capital, and used equipment and cast-off type from other Scripps newspapers. Dr. Earnest "Doc" Dozier, publisher of the *Dial*, dismissed the newcomer's physical assets as "a shirttail full of type."

The *Record* did not actively solicit advertising until circulation reached 1,500, but some local businesses—including The Hub, a clothing store, and McDonald's Chapel—placed advertising with the newcomer from the beginning.

By its first issue, published October 17, 1938, the *Record* could count 500 subscribers. More than 100 additional papers were sold on stands the first day. In just over a week, paid circulation doubled. A year later, in October 1939, the *Record* showed its first monthly profit—eight dollars.

By April 1941 the *Independent* had folded and the *Searchlight and Courier-Free Press* were sold to Red-

---

The Record Searchlight *will celebrate its 50th anniversary in 1988, but its predecessor, the* Shasta Courier, *goes back to the Gold Rush days. Since 1985 the newspaper had been published from this new, $8-million facility near the Twin View Boulevard/I-5 interchange.*

ding Record Inc. The transaction resulted in a merged *Record and Courier-Free Press* as an afternoon paper. The *Searchlight* was continued as a morning paper.

Rationing during World War II forced consolidation of the morning and afternoon papers into one edition, and thus the *Record Searchlight* was born.

Bodenhamer retired July 15, 1972, to be succeeded by Robert W. Edkin, present editor. Bostwick left the paper in 1950 to become business manager of the Ventura paper. His successor was Carey D. Guichard, who was succeeded by Larry Wakefield, the present business manager, in December 1979.

In the 1950s same-day carrier delivery was extended into eastern

Shasta, southern Siskiyou, and Trinity counties, and today carrier delivery covers an area of nearly 10,000 square miles.

From the beginning, the *Record Searchlight* has pursued a policy of aggressive newsgathering and vigorous editorial leadership. Early on, it campaigned against prostitution, gambling, and civic corruption, and, on a more positive note, on behalf of a countywide library. The newspaper has led the fights for several important annexations to Redding, and for public power, a county health department, a civic auditorium, and the Downtown Redding Mall.

It endorsed public development of Whiskeytown National Recreation Area and helped the 1974 passage of the Wild Rivers Act. A 1973 probe led to a Grand Jury accusation against the county assessor, and an extensive editorial campaign in 1977-1978 had major impact on county land-use and zoning policies and the drafting of a new general plan.

A week-long report on the area's economy in early 1985 led to a broad-based effort to diversify the region's boom-bust economy.

The newspaper co-sponsors several annual events including a Citizen of the Year Award, the Redding Marathon, and the Shasta Dixieland Jazz Festival.

In 1982 the newspaper moved to a new $8-million facility near the Twin View Boulevard/I-5 interchange.

McCOLLUM FUNDING

Three brothers, all raised and schooled in Redding, have brought together a combination of talents to provide a vital, but generally unseen, service to the citizens of Shasta County. Arranging financing and loan terms for real estate purchase or construction can be the critical step in a project, whether it be a new home or commercial construction.

Brothers Vernon M., Larry M., and I. Dennis McCollum in 1980 created a general partnership at 1525 Pine Street in Redding to offer the borrowing public what Vern calls a "best-type loan" for real estate and mobile ("manufactured home") loan transactions.

The business was initially operated by Larry and Vern, veterans of many years in the insurance, finance, and mortgage fields. Dennis, a partner in the business, is primarily engaged in the management of McCollum Realty and Development and McCollum Construction Company. Vern joined McCollum Funding on a full-time basis after his retirement in 1983 from Beneficial Corporation.

"We basically provide two services," Vern explains. "A lot of loans would qualify with any lender, but we put the borrower into a better loan than is available from traditional sources. Every lender has different criteria, which may be set by federal or state law for traditional lenders. We also can serve people who, because of personal problems or 'unreal guidelines,' cannot qualify for traditional funding. We have lenders who will give them an opportunity to buy."

The combination of talents available in McCollum Funding—licensed broker, licensed real estate agent, licensed contractor, notary public, licensed insurance agent—offers all essential services for a transaction. The firm is able to keep borrowers'

The three McCollum brothers (left to right), Dennis, Vern, and Larry, joined their combination of talents into McCollum Funding.

costs to a minimum through access to out-of-area lending sources and a program in which McCollum Funding does all the processing, verifications, title searches, and other functions that otherwise generate significant overhead cost.

While pointing out that all client relations are confidential, McCollum says, "In Redding alone, during 1985, $7 million of building costs resulted from our efforts." Total building permits for that period for single and multifamily and commercial construction were about $61.5 million.

The McCollum brothers are the sons of Ivan and Irene McCollum. Ivan grew up in the Oregon timber

industry and met Irene at Westwood in Lassen County, where her family was among the early pioneers of the community. In the mid-1940s they joined the "Westwood Migration" to Shasta County and all three boys, as well as a sister, Julie, were graduated from Shasta High School.

Three expansions of office space have occurred since the firm's opening, and McCollum Funding now has seven employees and expects continued growth in the coming years. "We work with people in the metropolitan areas, but none of us would move to a large city," Vern says. "Redding is home—we'll keep it that way."

SIMPSON PAPER COMPANY

One of the local area's major industries is the Simpson Paper Company's Shasta Mill, which provides steady, year-round employment for 600 people with a $29-million annual payroll.

Located at Anderson, the facility was built in 1964 and acquired by Simpson eight years later. Since then, the firm has invested $94 million to expand the mill, make it more productive, and meet environmental standards.

Although paper as we know it was created in 105 A.D. by the Chinese, today it requires massive machinery and advanced technology to manufacture this everyday necessity of life.

The consumption of paper reflects a country's standard of living and its level of literacy. America leads the world in producing 643 pounds per year for every man, woman, and child in the nation.

Shasta Mill produces both pulp

The block-long paper machine at the Simpson mill in Anderson is capable of producing a roll of coated paper up to 168 inches wide at a rate of 2,000-lineal-feet per minute.

and paper. The basic processes are simple. Pulp is manufactured by removing the cellulose from wood. Wood chips the size of a quarter are "cooked" with steam and chemicals, yielding cellulose fiber that becomes pulp; the other component of wood, called lignin, is burned as a fuel. Pulp is bleached with chemicals to attain a bright white color. All the chemicals used to make pulp are constantly recycled, and fresh chemicals are added to the process.

Simpson manufactures 250 tons of bleached kraft pulp daily, which then goes to the adjacent paper mill. There it is mixed with water and chemicals, then sprayed onto a continuously moving screen. At this point the sheet of paper is 99-percent water and one-percent wood fibers. The sheet is pressed, dried, and emerges from the paper machine at speeds up to 2,000 feet a minute, where it is wound onto rolls up to 60 inches in diameter. Shasta Mill has two paper machines: One produces a sheet 168 inches wide, the other 140 inches wide. From the paper machine the rolls go to the finishing department or to the firm's Ripon or San Gabriel, California, facilities where they are cut into smaller rolls or sheets. Shasta Mill products are shipped by truck and rail to customers all over the West.

The plant specializes in coated papers, which are used in high-quality

Mountains of wood chips continuously feed the Simpson Paper Company pulp mill, which in turn provides bleached kraft pulp for the adjacent paper mill.

printing jobs such as magazines and corporate annual reports. (Coating paper is similar to starching a man's shirt, in that clay and other substances are spread over the sheet and pressed to give a smooth, shiny surface.) Simpson produces paper coated on one or two sides. Coated one-side paper is used extensively in California for labels by the canned goods and wine industries. The corporation's other major local products include xerographic paper for photocopy machines and paper for bank checks.

Shasta Mill, which makes a substantial effort to protect the local environment and conserve natural resources, utilizes modern equipment to reduce emissions into the atmosphere—with special emphasis on minimizing the odor that comes from making pulp. It has over 30 permits to operate equipment of systems that discharge into the atmosphere. All these discharges meet the stringent limitations of the Shasta County District, as well as state and federal standards.

The mill uses 11.5 million gallons of water daily, which must be cleaned to remove impurities before discharge. Consequently, it has modern primary and secondary wastewater treatment facilities. A unique feature of Simpson's environmental protection program is the use of treated water to irrigate farm crops grown on a 400-acre ranch owned by the company. The irrigation system includes over 20,000 lineal feet of buried pipe, 450 valves, and over 100,000 feet of compressed-air lines to activate these valves. Groundwater quality and movement are monitored by 15 test wells and 40 observation wells.

Simpson conserves resources through the use of wood chips, the "leftovers" from making lumber and plywood, to make pulp. This utilization extends the value of timber

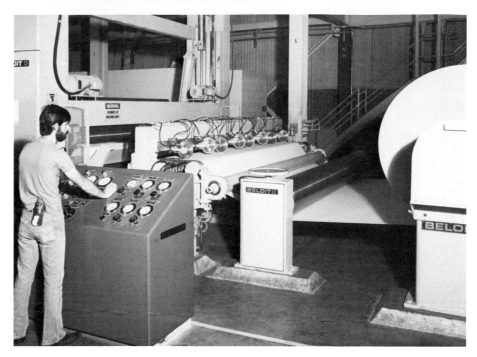

Technology is a major element in the operation of the high-speed paper machine, producing label stock for the state's wine and canning industries.

harvests and eliminates air pollution that would be caused by burning the chips. The firm buys these scraps from 14 sawmills and plywood plants in Northern California.

Another form of conservation is the $18.5-million cogeneration plant Simpson opened in 1983. The production of two types of energy— electricity and steam—from a single fuel, cogeneration is twice as efficient as production of a traditional electric generating plant. The Shasta facility burns natural gas in a huge jet engine that generates up to 39 megawatts of electricity, enough to meet the requirements of about 32,000 three-bedroom homes. The electricity is sold to a power com-

pany; and the waste heat from the turbine is used to produce steam for drying pulp and paper.

In addition to its $29-million annual payroll, Shasta Mill makes major contributions to the local economy through over one million dollars in annual tax payments and more than $12 million in purchases of local goods and services.

The plant is one of eight pulp and paper facilities operated by San Francisco-based Simpson Paper Company. The others are at Ripon, Eureka, and Pomona, California; Tacoma, Washington; Vicksburg, Michigan; Middletown, Ohio; and Miquon, Pennsylvania.

Huge rolls of paper taken from the paper machine must be cut to small sizes and rewound to fit on the printing presses of the customers of Simpson Paper Company.

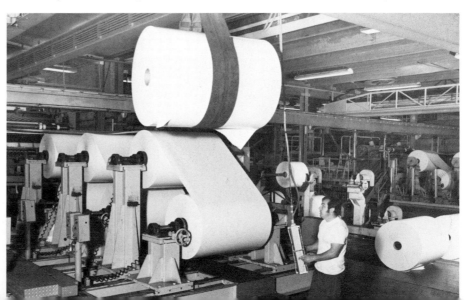

PEPSI COLA BOTTLING COMPANY

By March 16, 1933, the Great Depression had closed the banks in Shasta County and the rest of the nation, but that was of little concern to 24-year-old John Fitzpatrick. President Roosevelt's declaration of a national emergency and banking "holiday" had little impact on the son of a Churn Creek Bottom dairyman, who had no money anyway.

Fitzpatrick's interest that day centered on an offer from Senator John McColl to enter into a partnership, manufacturing and selling ice cream in Redding.

McColl owned McColl's Confectionery on Market Street, a typical soda fountain hangout for high school students of the 1930s. His duties in the legislature would occupy much of his time, and he needed help in his operation. He brought to the partnership the financing and an outlet for some of the production. Fitzpatrick brought experience in the refrigeration business, a few years as a foreman in a local creamery, and a background knowledge of the dairy industry gained from milking cows on his

When the new Pepsi Cola plant in Redding was opened in 1978, an estimated 15,000 people flocked to the Mountain Gate Industrial Park, where a full carnival and free rides were offered on the Pepsi site.

father's Churn Creek Bottom farm. He also brought a philosophy of fair dealing and superior products, ambition, and, perhaps, naive enthusiasm.

In a batch plant in a one-car garage behind the confectionery, Fitzpatrick manufactured about a dozen flavors of ice cream. He supplied the confectionery-soda fountain, then hired youngsters to pull wagons—packed with ice and salt to keep the ice cream frozen—through the neighborhoods shouting "Ice Cream! Ice Cream!" as Redding's summer thermometer soared over the 100-degree mark.

Within three years McColl & Fitzpatrick's (which later became McColl's Dairy Products, then McColl's) moved out of the garage-turned-ice-cream-plant and into a larger location near the Western Hotel on Oregon Street. Fitzpatrick opened retail distribution routes for both ice cream and milk, eventually capturing a major contract to supply the 5,000 workers building nearby Shasta Dam.

McColl died in an automobile accident while en route to legislative duties in 1938, and Fitzpatrick suffered the loss of a close friend, business partner, and mentor. He continued with the dairy business in partnership with Mrs. McColl until he bought her share in 1958.

In 1952 McColl's had again moved to larger quarters, a new plant on Angelo Avenue, in an era in which innovation and progress

Marie and John Fitzpatrick, Sr., greeted 700 customers at a dinner during the 1972 dedication of the new Pepsi plant in Redding.

were essential to maintaining the firm's now-strong area position in the industry.

Fitzpatrick was the first dairyman in the state to abandon the 10-gallon milk cans when he began hauling milk from the dairies to the plant in stainless steel tank trucks and helped his producers finance steel tanks at the dairy. Cottage cheese, buttermilk, and sour cream were added to the company's line of products. Glass bottles were abandoned, and all milk was packaged and sold in paper cartons. Pasteurization had been adopted by the innovative Fitzpatrick almost 15 years earlier.

In 1966 he purchased the Pepsi Cola franchise for Shasta, Trinity, Tehama, and Glenn counties, and Chico at an estate sale.

Under Fitzpatrick management the Pepsi plant soon outgrew its facilities, and in 1978 it moved to the Mountain Lakes Industrial Park north of Redding in a new $2-million plant providing the only Pepsi canning facility between the Bay Area and Yakima, Washington.

John and Marie Fitzpatrick have retired from active operation of the business he founded. They have passed the reins to sons Bill (left), John (right), and Jerry (inset).

With a capacity of 20,000 cases of cans and 5,000 cases of bottles every two shifts daily, the firm is also franchised to produce the Slice products from Pepsi, and contracts with various other drink manufacturers to can or bottle their products.

John Fitzpatrick worked hard to overcome what he felt was the major failing of businessmen—an unwillingness to meet an obligation to be involved in their community.

In the early 1940s he became an active member and president of the Redding Rotary Club and president of the Greater Redding Chamber of Commerce. In the late 1940s the civic-minded businessman helped enact a one-percent sales tax to help finance city operations, despite opposition from many of his business

In 1952 McColl's Dairy Products outgrew its quarters and moved to this plant on Angelo Avenue. There John Fitzpatrick implemented a variety of innovations, which were to make the firm a leader in the industry.

peers. Subsequently serving as chairman of a referendum committee that fought city plans to close Benton Airport, he succeeded in retaining it and forcing the city to undertake improvements. He was a charter member of the Asphalt Cowboys, active in California Kamloops, Grand Jury foreman in 1955, and active in Republican party politics throughout most of his business career.

Two of Fitzpatrick's three sons, John and Bill, had joined his business in the early 1960s. John, a graduate engineer with a master's degree in business administration, slowly assumed management of the dairy operations as his father backed away from day-to-day operations. Bill, with training in dairy science from the University of California at Davis, initially was involved in the dairy; after the Pepsi acquisition he concentrated his

efforts on developing that venture.

During the 1970s the founder reduced his role in the company enterprises as son John guided the dairy operations and Bill directed the Pepsi Cola activities, with the family selling McColl's to Crystal Cream & Butter Company of Sacramento in 1985. Later that year Bill retired from the management of the Pepsi operations, and John assumed that responsibility. Another brother, Jerry, who resides in Marin County, is active as secretary and a board member of the Redding Pepsi plant.

The family is also currently involved in the operation of the John Fitzpatrick & Sons data-processing service for area firms.

The senior Fitzpatrick and his wife, Marie, now enjoy the leisure, travel, and recreation earned through decades of struggle and devotion to his family, business, and community.

SUNSET PLASTICS, INC.

Charles M. Ehn, who migrated from Southern California, started his own business in 1968 and today heads Sunset Plastics, Inc., manufacturer of top-of-the-line fiberglass shower stalls, bathtubs, tub/shower combinations, whirlpool baths, and spas.

The founder was raised on a ranch in the San Fernando Valley, where his father was a professional trapper and cattle rancher. Charles worked at a variety of trades—truck owner/operator, livestock feeder, assembly line worker, foreman at General Motors, and mold maker of fiberglass parts for aircraft—in the San Fernando area until a vacation trip to Northern California in 1965 convinced him that he and his family should move there.

Ehn was employed as a laborer at the Lewiston Fish Hatchery and later as a construction worker for the Kimberly-Clark Corporation pulp and paper mill at Anderson. After the mill was completed, he began work with a fiberglass shower manufacturer in Central Valley and rose to the position of foreman. When his recommendations for improved product quality and sales went unheeded, he changed jobs to work for a boat manufacturer in the tooling department and became superintendent of production. He started working nights and weekends using his experiences in fiberglassing and mold making to launch his own business.

In 1968 the entrepreneur and his family built their first mold for shower stalls in a rickety barn behind their home on Sunset Lane in Anderson. Using plywood, putty, and rigid foam blocks, they built a full-size model "plug" of the shower stall they wanted, then laboriously sanded, polished, and buffed it to its final shape and appearance. The Ehns then sprayed fiberglass and polyester resins over the waxed plug to create the mold on which they

ultimately cast their first shower stall. This original mold is still in production.

Although the home construction market was flourishing, Ehn found sales hard to come by. "I had no reputation and no established place of business. Wholesalers wouldn't buy from me. They were used to dealing with established manufacturers," he recalls. In an old pickup loaded with stalls, the undaunted business owner started driving the highways from Anderson to Reno to Klamath Falls, Oregon, looking for customers. "I would find a house being built and stop by and try to make a sale," he says. "I sold a few to lumberyards, but they didn't want to alienate their regular wholesale suppliers."

Sales slowly developed, and what was to become Sunset Plastics was under way. After moving to a rented storage facility in Central Valley, the firm added the first tub/shower mold to its line. The next move was to a "tin building" on South Street in Anderson, then to larger quarters on Eastside Road—near the boat manufacturer for whom he had previously worked. In a symbolic relationship, Ehn did the final castings on boat molds in exchange for a discounted price for materials he needed for his tub and shower manufacturing. The business had by then grown large enough to warrant further expansion, so his brother, Harry, joined him to form a

A truck, loaded with the bulky but lightweight Sunset Plastic tubs and showers, leaves the plant on a delivery run. Photo circa 1976

A production worker sprays a mixture of chopped fiberglass and polyester resins on a tub mold being produced at the Sunset Plastics, Inc., factory.

partnership.

The next move was into a structure that had previously served as a supermarket and later a truck shop. In exchange for two months free rent, Ehn and his family cleaned out the old building—which still serves today as the production shop for Sunset Plastics, incorporated in 1970. Four years later, on adjacent property purchased by the firm, 10,000 square feet of offices, show-

Charles M. Ehn, founder of Sunset Plastics, Inc., manufacturer of fiberglass shower stalls, bathtubs, tub/shower combinations, whirlpool baths, and spas.

The new office and showroom of Sunset Plastics in Anderson.

rooms, and warehouse were constructed. Those facilities were supplemented in 1985 with another new building of approximately 14,500 square feet.

Sunset's first brochure listed four styles of shower and one tub/shower combination. Today the company has 27 shower models; 13 tub/shower combinations; 8 tubs; and 22 "Regency Tubs," a deluxe line of over-size tubs with optional whirlpool fittings. The firm has over 200 molds in production.

All Sunset Plastic products are made by the in-line production method, Ehn relates, explaining that

he has shunned automation and the lower production costs in order to maintain the quality and versatility he seeks. "If we are lucky, we can make two per day from any mold, and we have many identical molds. A lot of our work is in customized colors that the high-volume manufacturers don't want to make. The customer may even send us a sample of wallpaper or tile and ask us to match it."

Ehn explains that the style of the products is dictated by market demands and for comfort and beauty, and he has refused to restyle the tubs and showers for ease of shipping. "Ninety percent are shipped on our own trucks, and it is very expensive," he says, adding that many of the volume manufacturers design their tubs for ease of manufacturing

and "nest" them during shipping, saving space and costs but limiting their style. "We are lucky if we can get 35 on a truck and trailer, including loading them over the cab."

According to Ehn the firm ships about 1,000 units per month—with a crew ranging from 35 to 65, fluctuating with the seasonal rise and fall of home construction. Associated in the business with him and Harry, who is vice-president, are Harry's son, Harry Jr., in the shipping department; Charles' wife, Mayme, corporate secretary; son Chuck, corporate treasurer; daughters Catherine E. Mayer, who handles all advertising, Cynthia Barwick, retail sales representative, Julie Tietzel, showroom manager; and daughter-in-law Bridgett, office manager.

SHARRAH DUNLAP AND ASSOCIATES, INC.

Northern California's most significant attribute is its outstanding natural beauty.

Protecting this beauty while providing for the growth necessary for a vital economic base is the challenge facing this region, according to Sharrah Dunlap and Associates, Inc.

Sharrah Dunlap deals with this challenge daily in the practice of civil and structural engineering, surveying, and land and environmental planning. The firm believes that development should be shaped to fit the area rather than reshaping the area to fit preconceived ideas of development.

In more than 20 years of existence, Sharrah Dunlap has been responsible for the design of residential subdivisions of more than 6,000 lots, large mobile home parks, and many commercial sites. It has provided the engineering for numerous structures, including schools and public buildings in virtually every community in the North State.

A major influence on the firm's operations is the strong identification of its principals with the region. John Sharrah cites his role in the acquisition and development of Anderson River Park as one of his most significant accomplishments. John Dunlap served as a member of the board responsible for the expansion and modernization of the Centerville-Placer area water system. Frank Sawyer and Eihnard Diaz have been intensively involved in efforts to effect desirable economic growth. This is in addition to all of them serving on other community-focused committees.

Recent representative projects utilizing the capabilities of the firm include the 17,000-foot Upper Churn Creek sewer trunk line and assess-

ment district, the 110-lot Gold Hills and the 204-lot Mary Lake residential developments in Redding, and the 115-lot River Park subdivision in Anderson.

The firm performed the site location studies for the new regional sewer plant and the structural design for the 100,000-square-foot regional postal facility to be built in Redding and the $4-million jail for Siskiyou County. In addition to large projects, Sharrah Dunlap specializes in the smaller jobs such as lot splits and parcel surveys that, in the aggregate, have a substantial

Eihnard Diaz (right) and John Sharrah at the Mary Lake Subdivision in Redding.

impact on the character of growth in the area.

The desirability of Northern California as a place to live and to raise families is given as the principal reason the firm has been able to attract and maintain a staff of approximately 20 experienced professionals. They share the principals' commitment that economic development must be of a nature to enhance the quality of life. And their work substantiates this commitment.

Frank Sawyer (right) and John Dunlap at the U.S. Forest Service Center in Redding.

FOOTHILL DISTRIBUTING COMPANY, INC.

A five-year search for a beer distributorship was centered in Los Angeles for Dick and Mary Jane Tews and led them as far away as Scottsbluff, Nebraska, before the couple located in Redding—where they have become a permanent part of the community and have been named Business of the Month by both the Greater Redding Chamber of Commerce and the Redding Trade Club.

Tews began work for Anheuser Busch Brewing Company in Denver in 1962, then moved to Montana, where he became district manager. He was married to Mary Jane, whom he had met in Colorado, and who became the teacher of a seven-grade, one-room school near Great Falls.

After transfers to San Diego and Los Angeles with Anheuser Busch, the couple began a search for a distributorship in a suitable location and with good potential. In 1972 they purchased the Superior Beverage Corporation from Al Huckins, later closing the Red Bluff office and centering all operations in Redding. "We had five employees when we started, and we now have 44. Our sales have gone from 200,000 cases per year to well over one million cases annually. Foothill's fleet has also grown from a total of seven vehicles in 1972 to 50 in 1986," Dick Tews says.

In October 1978 the firm moved into its present facilities in the Mountain Lake Industrial Park. The facility, which has already undergone one expansion, includes 40,000 square feet of space for offices, com-

puter systems, training rooms for salesmen, storage, shops, and truck maintenance.

With Budweiser as its flagship brand, Foothill distributes all Anheuser Busch products to over 600 retail licensees in Shasta, Trinity, and Tehama counties. The wholesaler has recently created a specialty products division to market its imported beers, mineral waters, wine, and soft drink items.

Both Tews are enthusiastic participants in community activities. Mary Jane is in her fourth year as a director of the Greater Redding Chamber of Commerce, and also serves as a member of the executive committee of the Private Industry Council, the Economic Development Corporation board, and the Redding

Mary Jane and Dick Tews of Foothill Distributing Company have been active participants in Shasta County community affairs while managing the distributorship they acquired in 1972.

Medical Center board of directors. Dick is associated with the Lions Club, Elks Lodge, and Moose Lodge, and formerly served on the Redding Airport Commission.

Foothill Distributing Company, Inc., has been deeply involved in sponsorship of the local "Operation Alert" alcohol awareness program, including programs in the schools designed to educate students in the use of alcohol and to emphasize that, if it is used, moderation is essential.

Tews is an avid amateur pilot who performs in many air shows, flying his T-34 military trainer aircraft—painted in Budweiser colors—to various areas of the country. The aircraft, dubbed the "Flying Beer Can" by his aerial associates, has the Budweiser logo painted conspicuously on its side.

The entrepreneurs' daughter, Lynn, is studying communications and business at Chico State University, and has been involved in the operation of Foothill Distributing Company, Inc., during summer months for several years.

Dick Tews of Redding is a regular participant in air shows around the country in the Flying Beer Can, a converted military trainer. Tews demonstrated aerobatics at recent Redding air shows.

CITIZENS UTILITIES COMPANY OF CALIFORNIA

A staff of 150 at Citizens Utilities Company's California headquarters in Redding provide support services for seven operating districts. Photo by Peter Aaron/ESTO

Citizens Utilities Company is headquartered in Stamford, Connecticut, and provides telephone, electric, gas, water, and wastewater services to more than 300,000 customers in 500 communities and 10 states. Its offspring—the Redding-based Citizens Utilities Company of California—is involved in telephone operations from Solano and Sacramento counties to Siskiyou, Modoc, and Humboldt counties.

In Shasta County the firm provides the telephone link to the outside world for communities from Manzanita Lake to the Fall River Area, and along Highway 299 from Palo Cedro to Round Mountain and Big Bend, serving approximately 6,000 families and businesses from the remote mountainous regions to Palo Cedro.

Citizens' district offices in Alturas and Susanville provide service for the McCloud area in southern Siskiyou County, most of Lassen County, all of Modoc County, and northern Plumas and eastern Tehama Counties, spreading its telephonic web over most non-Forest Service lands in northeastern California.

Commercial phone service in Lassen, Plumas, and Modoc counties had its origin in the California and Oregon Telegraph Company of 1892—which provided telegraph services between Reno, Nevada, and Lakeview, Oregon, via Susanville, Adin, and Alturas, with some telephone service in Modoc County. Other telephone and telegraph operations developed to provide services to roughly the same area and to provide train dispatching services. In 1914 the California and Oregon Telegraph Company emerged as the survivor of the many competing services.

In 1927 the organization purchased the Bass Telephone Lines, a privately owned system extending from Redding to Fall River Mills in Shasta County. Then, in 1929, the combined properties were acquired by the Public Utilities of California Corporation, which in 1949 changed its name to Citizens Utilities Company of California.

"It may be surprising," division manager John Rutherford says, "but historically, the rural areas generally developed telephone systems earlier than the cities that enjoyed quick mail service and short distances for face-to-face meetings." He continues: "Because the rural people had travel problems and poor mail delivery, they started telephone co-ops. The

Ray Coffelt owned and operated the Bear Creek-Millville phone lines from 1946 until 1956, when he sold to the predecessor of Citizens Utilities. Two years later he joined the firm to begin a 20-year career.

farmers got together and strung telephone lines as the top wire on their fences. It was a casual organization; they interconnected over the years, eventually hiring managers and forming stock companies owned by subscribers. Slowly these operations grew to the point where they were difficult to manage, and the subscribers sold to companies like Citizens."

At the conclusion of World War II, much of rural Shasta County was still dependent upon these farmer-originated "barbed-wire phone companies." In 1946, when the area was considered a "nuisance territory," Ray Coffelt paid Melvin Hawes $100 for what was known as the Bear Creek/Millville Lines, paid $120 to a Citizens Utilities subsidiary for what is now part of the Bella Vista exchange, and was given a part of the Bell System's Anderson exchange.

The agreement was approved by the Railroad Commission, predecessor to the Public Utilities Commission, and Coffelt was in business as a "model" independent with about 10 subscribers in Millville, five in Palo Cedro, and approximately a half-dozen farmer lines. His wife, Rika, was the operator.

Ten years later Coffelt had built some 700 miles of line and expanded to 115 subscribers. He sold the sys-

Oregon Street, and in 1963 relocated to the present site at 1035 Placer Street; subsequent additions to the latter office resulted in today's 49,300-square-foot facility.

The headquarters provides support services for all seven operating districts in California: Elk Grove in Sacramento County; Susanville, serving Lassen and portions of Plumas and Tehama counties; Rio Vista in Solano County; Ferndale in Humboldt County; Alturas (most of Modoc County); Burney (portions of Shasta, Lassen, Modoc, and Siskiyou counties); and Palo Cedro (portions of eastern Shasta County).

Approximately 150 employees make up the headquarters support staff, providing accounting, engi-

This digital switching system was installed in the Burney area in 1986 and provides the most modern services available.

neering, data-management, customer services, and personnel functions. The Redding office also provides a purchasing and warehousing function for the districts.

Citizens has aggressively kept its equipment modern and efficient. A digital microwave system provides two routes between Redding and Reno for long distance calls, intertying with AT&T and Pacific Bell at both terminals and providing a loop to handle calls in the event of a malfunction in any portion of the system.

By the end of 1986 all offices in the Burney area were also converted to digital equipment from the old electromechanical switching devices. The Palo Cedro equipment will be replaced in mid-1987. This modern equipment converts the human voice to a computer-generated "bit stream," or series of numbers that are translated back to a voice pattern at the receiving end.

The days of the crank-operated magneto telephone have been replaced by the modern computer age.

Fully automated digital switching centers are the latest equipment being installed by Citizens Utilities Company for a telephone system that once was partially strung on farmers' fence posts, and later depended upon these 1950-era "central" operators.

tem to what is now Citizens Utilities for $41,500 in 1956, went to work for the firm two years later, and continued working for it for 20 years.

Citizens Utilities Company of California was incorporated in 1927 in San Francisco as Public Utilities of California Corporation and changed to the current name in 1949. That year its headquarters was moved to Redding in facilities above the Roy F. Brown Furniture Store on

KMS RESEARCH LABORATORIES, INC.

Responding to the public's concern for health—not merely cosmetic appearance of health—has been one of the keys to success of KMS Research Laboratories, Inc.

"Most hair products are considered conditioners," according to Jamey Mazzotta, the firm's president and director of research. "They merely keep the hair in its same condition. But all our products are reconstructive—they don't just stay on the surface. KMS' philosophy is that hair, as living protein, can ingest and digest material through surface application. In the laboratory, we can find the added protein from (applied) KMS products all the way down to the cortical fiber in the middle of the hair shaft."

Mazzotta was senior chemist for a major hair care manufacturer in 1975 when he and two partners launched the new line of reconstructive hair products, which has achieved worldwide acceptance under the KMS label.

KMS president Jamey Mazzotta leads the field in the ground-effect road racer, which he drives regularly during the summer circuit.

For the first few years KMS and its 10 employees were located in a rented automotive sales building at 1729 California Street in Redding. In 1978 a striking new 25,000-square-foot building was constructed on a hillside overlooking the intersection of Highway 299 and Deschutes Road in Bella Vista. The firm quickly outgrew that facility, and the blending and formulation of materials was moved back to Redding in a 25,000-square-foot structure on Railroad Avenue. The firm's laboratory for product formulation and testing is also housed at the Railroad Avenue location.

The Bella Vista site remained as company headquarters and offices, as well as providing final packaging and shipping operations. In early 1986 the firm began plans for a new, combined facility of 100,000 to 150,000 square feet in the Mountain Lakes Industrial Park. Employment at that time was approximately 75 persons, including chemists, technicians, and production line workers, hired locally and trained to KMS criteria for quality control.

The hair care industry has for

Jamey Mazzotta is president and director of research of KMS Research Laboratories, producer of hair care products sold worldwide.

years used deoxyribonucleic acids (DNA) and ribonucleic acids (RNA), extracted from yeast, as a hair conditioner, and it is effective. KMS, however, has developed a process allowing it to extract even greater nutrients from the yeast—primarily the proteins found in the nucleus of the yeast cells. "The nucleoproteins reconstruct the texture and the integrity of the hair," Mazzotta explains. "They don't merely settle on the surface; they are ingested by the hair and supplement the normal feeding of the hair by the body."

Another technological advance developed at KMS is Prolimin-49®, derived from bee pollen through a series of hydrolysis and extraction processes to produce a material that not only provides hair nutrition but also controls the amount of moisture in the hair.

Mazzotta attributes the firm's success to product quality combined with a strong and innovative marketing program designed to be attractive both to distributors and

Bottles bearing the distinctive KMS logo are filled by production workers at the Bella Vista plant.

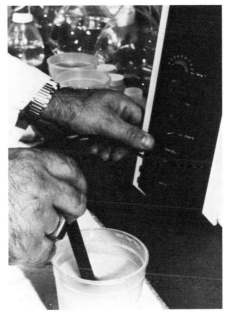

Repeated quality-control checks are made on all hair care products produced at the Shasta County facilities of KMS Laboratories.

hair salons. The hair stylists are ultimately the key to consumer use and acceptance, he notes. They must first learn the potentials of the product and how to apply it and why it is effective.

Although the hair stylists buy the product for their own use, Mazzotta says that 75 percent of the KMS sales are by hair stylists who sell the products to customers for home use. The items are not sold through drugstores, supermarkets, or other retail channels, and can be obtained only from a beauty salon.

While some of the ingredients are purchased from chemical manufacturers, the key elements—nucleoproteins and Prolimin-49—are produced in the KMS labs in Redding. Mixing of ingredients is subject to careful quality control, both regarding weights and measurements of various ingredients and close attention to such factors as mixing temperatures and time. Every batch is subject to testing, once on the day of manufacture and again three days later as it is packaged. Records of all processing are maintained for several years.

"We may not be the flashiest or the most avant guarde (in our image), but the hairdressers know they can depend on KMS—it works," Mazzotta says.

KMS Research Laboratories, Inc., manufactures the firm's products in Canada, England, and Australia; and they are sold in Europe, Hong Kong, most of Malaysia, Thailand, Puerto Rico, the West Indies, and

This striking office and plant in Bella Vista houses a portion of the facilities of KMS Research Laboratories, Inc.

West Africa. Most of the foreign sales have evolved from inquiries of visitors to the United States who use the product here, according to Bill Bengtsson, vice-president and general manager. KMS' line includes products for shampoos, reconstruction, and styling, Bengtsson points out, and all the overseas sales are of the same product under the same label.

Chemistry and biology are not Mazzotta's only interests. He is a professional auto racer and winner of the 1985 Northwest Pacific Championship for Formula 2000 road racers. He developed a love of high-speed automobiles in high school, and now drives vehicles prepared by Proformula, Inc., of Sacramento. Mazzotta says Proformula's maintenance crew will generally spend up to 40 hours preparing the factory-built racers for an event. With ground-effect styling, the vehicles are capable of speeds up to 170 miles per hour. His wife, Cheryl, and sons James, Zacery, and Hawk join him on the spring and summer racing circuit as fans and supporters while he is driving under the KMS banner.

REDDING ELEMENTARY SCHOOL DISTRICT

By today's standards, the Redding Elementary School District wasn't much when it was established in 1856 as the Canon House District.

The first teacher was Anne Reid, who was paid $35 a month for the three-month school session and whose descendants still live in Shasta County.

What is now Redding was an uncleared wilderness of pine, oak, manzanita, and chapparal. By 1871 there were only 16 students enrolled, and the average daily attendance was nine.

One of the first students, a boy selected for his relative size and maturity, was asked by the teacher to bring a gun to school—for protection against possible Indian attacks, although records indicate the first Indians to enter the school did so as students less than 15 years later.

By 1872 a community had been established and enrollment jumped to 91, clearly overloading the one-room school. A new facility was opened the next year on Pine street between Placer and Yuba streets to house the overflow from the Canon House school (which had been physically relocated to an area called Canyon Bottom a few years prior).

In 1875 the district was renamed Reading, after the community founder, but later changed to Redding, the name the Central Pacific Railroad had given to the community to honor one of the railroad's land agents. By 1881 further population increases forced the community to approve $10,000 in bonds to build a brick schoolhouse on donated land at the intersection of Pine and Eureka Way. Classes were conducted

---

The brick building (left), erected in 1881, was supplemented in 1895 with the frame classroom facility to cope with enrollment growth at the Pine Street school. Courtesy, Shasta Historical Society

on the site of the second Pine Street school until 1967, and the original Pine Street school became known as "Little Pine."

In 1895 an $8,000 bond issue financed construction of a frame classroom building adjacent to the brick Pine Street school. By 1902 enrollment had grown to 766 students and "Little Pine" had worn out. Local citizens living on the west side of the railroad tracks wanted a new school in their neighborhood, but the deed restrictions forced the school district to rebuild on the "Little Pine" site. In a Solomon-like decision, a $20,000 bond issue financed rebuilding of "Little Pine" as a frame schoolhouse; a new brick school, called the West Side Grammar, was built; and the facility at Pine and Eureka Way became known as the East Side Grammar School.

The district finally abandoned the second Pine Street school site in 1967. The sturdy brick and concrete

"Little Pine" served the children and citizens of Redding for most of the community's existence. In the early 1900s a bond issue helped rebuild it, as shown here with students of the day outside the facility. Courtesy, Shasta Historical Society

building had been designated as an air raid shelter during World War II, but was declared inadequate as a school because of state earthquake standards. It was sold and is still in use today as a center for restaurants, professional and service offices, and other businesses.

Donated land, funds, and labor were the keys to the early development of the school district and the physical plants. The students were expected to contribute more than just their personal learning efforts. Better students helped those in difficulty (and undoubtedly strengthened their own learning by doing so). Teachers and administrators accepted the unwritten rule for "volunteers" for after-school activities.

The 1960s were, perhaps, the toughest of times for the district. The post-World War II baby boom clogged the classrooms, and funds simply were inadequate. Five efforts by the district to enact an override tax failed. As the funding dwindled, the end of the 1960s saw enrollments also fall to a low of 2,000 students in 1982. Schools were pared back, reorganized, or closed.

Today the enrollment is again increasing, with about 2,600 students in the district, compared to the peak of 3,700 in 1966-1967, and ex-

pected to grow at a rate of 4 to 5 percent annually over the next eight years. District master plans show a need to construct at least two more schools as well as adding classrooms at all existing schools.

Current schools include Sequoia Middle School, for sixth, seventh, and eighth grades, and Cypress, Juniper, Manzanita, BonnyView, and Sycamore, all for kindergarten to fifth grade. The Live Oak School, which had opened for seventh- and eighth-graders in 1966 and was closed in 1975 when enrollment dropped, was being leased to the Shasta County Office of Education in 1986 but is also a candidate for reopening in the near future.

"Today we must depend upon the state to sell bonds for school construction," William Kipp, district superintendent, says. "Those dis-

tricts with the most unhoused students get the first priority." He explains that state funds have been secured for reconstruction of the Cypress, Sequoia, and Manzanita schools to upgrade the existing facilities.

Additional state funds will be needed for classroom construction, but Kipp feels that the Redding district is in a good position to qualify. "As we look to the future," Kipp says, "education seems bright. We are getting more attention, more money, and lots of support. Student achievement, as measured by state and nationally standardized test scores, has been steadily increasing for the past few years. Salaries have been raised to a competitive level to attract and retain talented people. We're providing quality education and looking at expanding our instructional programs to provide students with the necessary skills for the twenty-first century."

The West Side School, built near the site of the present library, was created in 1902 as the result of pressure from citizens living west of the railroad tracks in Redding. Courtesy, Shasta Historical Society

NORTHERN CALIFORNIA PLASTIC SURGERY MEDICAL GROUP, INC.

The challenging care of human deformity and disability has led T.R. Knapp, M.D., from Keene, New Hampshire, to Florida, California, the South Pacific, Africa, and South America, but it is Redding and the surrounding North State area that since 1981 has had the primary benefit of his expertise and skills in the field of plastic surgery.

The New Hampshire boy who "always wanted to be a surgeon" was, at the University of Florida, named the graduate with the "most promise for becoming a physician of the highest type," and while interning at the University of Washington, was honored for his "clinical ability and humanitarian concern."

Knapp began his private practice in Eureka in 1977 and while practicing there was instrumental in developing Vector Health Programs—a not-for-profit organization providing free medical service for North Coast residents afflicted with craniofacial anomalies or severe arthritic or injury problems of the hands and upper limbs.

He shifted his practice from Humboldt County to Redding in 1981, becoming only the second plastic surgeon to practice in the area. Two years later he established the office of the Northern California Plastic Surgery Medical Group in the Clairmont Doctors Park adjacent to Mercy Medical Center. With Redding as a medical hub for a large geographical area, Knapp performs nearly 400 major surgeries per year and consults with or treats about 100 other patients per week. This office-based surgical facility, specifically designed for outpatient treatment, was the first fully accredited ambulatory surgery unit in the medical service area and has been accepted by all medical insurance agencies and Medicare.

Knapp's efforts also enabled the facility to become one of the first

All appropriate traditional hospital services are available in the outpatient surgery facility, although patients normally remain for only a few hours.

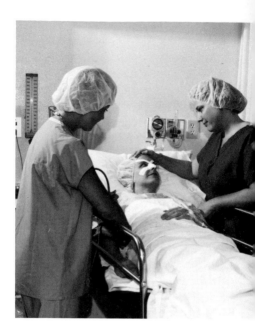

office-based surgery centers in the state to have outside peer review of the medical treatment provided. Under the program initiated by Knapp, every month a group of qualified nurses representing the County Medical Society reviews the medical services provided by the center and reports to its parent organization and to Knapp in a procedure designed to retain confidentiality of medical records while assuring quality of treatment.

According to Knapp, the ambula-

tory surgery unit has three advantages over traditional hospitalization. Medical care is less expensive, operations are more efficient as a result of specially trained personnel and design of the facilities for specific purposes, and confidentiality—of particular concern in cosmetic surgery—can be maintained.

The center's 3,600-square-foot upstairs area provides administrative facilities, rooms for patient examination, audiovisual equipment for patient education programs, facilities to televise and record operative procedures, and data-processing equipment. The 2,000-square-foot lower

This modern solar-heated office complex was completed in 1983 to house Northern California Plastic Surgery Medical Group, Inc. The facility was especially designed for outpatient surgery treatment.

level houses the fully equipped surgical suite, a three-bed recovery room, central delivery systems for oxygen and anesthetics, backup diesel electrical systems, and central surgical supply facilities.

A computer is also being developed to assist in some surgical processes. A program has been designed that allows the computer to "digitalize" an image of the patient's face, projecting it onto a video screen. The surgeon can then experiment on the projected image with various surgical changes and determine the cosmetic results to be expected. According to Knapp, this is a new tool, not yet fully developed, but one that he expects to be of significant future value to the surgeon and to patients.

Although cosmetic surgery may be the fastest-growing element of plastic surgery, Knapp says that the local area has need for an enormous amount of reconstructive hand surgery, either due to injury or arthritis, facial surgery to overcome birth defects, surgery in connection with tumor removal, and repair of severe injuries from accidents.

"A plastic surgeon is, perhaps, more intimately involved with the psychological aspects of care than any branch of medicine other than pure psychiatry," states Knapp. "We are trying to achieve something beyond pure technology—satisfying a person's expectations—and that often goes beyond the physical results."

Much of Knapp's medical training and skills have been devoted to providing treatment to those unable to pay for the basic services. He has been active in a Shasta County program with California Children's Services that provides treatment for children born with severe craniofacial birth defects—one out of every 1,000 live births. Knapp is also the founder and coordinator of the North Central Craniofacial Anomalies Panel, a group of medical specialists that coordinates the complex treatment that may involve reconstruction of the skull, cleft lip and palate, ears, and mouth—sometimes all for the same patient—requiring each specialist to integrate his or her work into the overall sequence of treatment. California Children's Services, a state-supported program, pays all costs if the patient is uninsured.

Knapp is also an active participant and former board member of

Interplast, Inc., which, through the donated services of American plastic surgeons, provides medical treatment of patients and training of physicians and surgeons in developing nations. Since 1973 Knapp, under the Interplast aegis, has worked and taught in Western Samoa; Mexicali, Mexico; Lesotho and Botswana, Africa; Cuenca, Equador; and Tacna and Iquitos, Peru.

"The strength of plastic surgery lies in its broad range of applications—cosmetic, industrial accidents (primarily to the hand), arthritis, restorative surgery, and overcoming birth defects," Knapp says.

Regarding his current efforts with Interplast and other humanitarian organizations, he says, "I just enjoy doing it. Any person who derives his living from a community should put something back into it. Most good businesses behave that way."

T.R. Knapp, M.D., directs activities at the Northern California Plastic Surgery Medical Group and regularly makes his skills available to U.S. and foreign citizens who would not be able to afford reconstructive surgery.

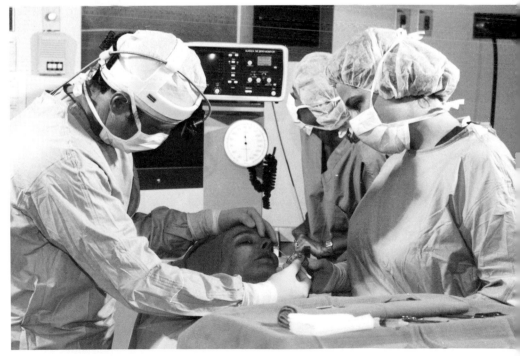

Less expensive than traditional hospitalization and designed for the type of surgery that will occur there, the Northern California Plastic Surgery Medical Group facility is fully accredited and Medicare certified.

SKYWAY RECREATION PRODUCTS

Charles Raudman, president of Skyway Recreation Products, has led his firm to prominence in the field of bicycle wheel manufacture and sales.

Charles Raudman and Skyway Recreation Products did not invent the wheel, but their improvements in its manufacture and design have led the firm to a prominent position in world cycling. Skyway Recreation Products and its associated corporations are the world's major supplier of bicycle wheels, with a technologically superior product that has caught the fancy of several industries.

Raudman was an engineering troubleshooter for a Burbank, California, manufacturer of hydraulic equipment in 1961 when he formed Skyway Machine Inc. to produce parts for the aerospace industry. Nine years later the entrepreneur, a former professional motorcycle racer, designed and produced an effective muffler and spark arrester that did not noticeably reduce engine power. Once patented, sales for the muffler soared as most major manufacturers sought it for original equipment on their off-road motorcycles, and the

California Department of Motor Vehicles required it to meet strict sound-level requirements in California.

BMX, or Bicycle Moto Cross racing, was coming into its own in the mid-1970s, luring youths to race over rugged trails on specially designed bicycles—much in the same manner as off-road motorbikes, but relying on leg power. A major problem was the wheels—which tended to break down under the torture of the off-road courses.

After 20 months of experimenting, Skyways developed a plastic wheel made of a blend of two patented DuPont materials. With extreme care and quality control in manufacture, the marketed wheel was lighter than either steel or aluminum, but stronger and more flexible. Raudman said a sample of the early wheel, marketed as Tuff Wheel I, is in the Smithsonian Institution as one of the most significant achievements in plastics uses in more than

30 years.

In 1977 Raudman moved the operations to Redding, where he constructed a 36,000-square-foot manufacturing facility that has already undergone one major expansion.

Although Tuff Wheel I was dominating the market, Skyways soon introduced Tuff Wheel II—lighter, stronger, and able to be modified to various braking systems and hubs sought by the BMX enthusiasts. The superiority of the Skyway wheels developed entire new markets, as manufacturers of lawn mowers, ultra-light aircraft, wheelchairs, and others saw the value of the quality product.

Today Skyway parts are included as original equipment on street and off-road bicycles worldwide; and the firm is marketing complete bikes, bearing the company label and primarily constructed of Skyway parts, as well as accessories such as goggles, masks, brake parts, pedals, and various other products.

With 70 employees, the Redding facility is producing 70,000 to 100,000 wheels per month, and is the major nylon bike wheel manufacturer in the world. Near London, England, a Skyway manufacturing plant has been established to service the Western European market. Around the Pacific Rim, from Australia to Japan, Skyway parts are in use.

Raudman has continued as president of the firm. John Raudman, his brother, serves as vice-president, and Dean Ellison is secretary/treasurer. Raudman's son Craig is the plant superintendent, while younger son Chris, who was ranked fifth in the world as a BMX competitor at age 18, is molding plant supervisor.

HANES INCORPORATED

Roy Hanes laid the foundation for Hanes incorporated in 1947, when he purchased two floor-sanding machines and a polisher from his employer, Ralph Livingston, for $757.05. Hanes continued to sand subflooring on linoleum jobs for Livingston, and began finishing hardwood floors for other contractors.

Hanes had moved to Redding in 1937 with his wife, Theo, and their daughter, Dona, to work on Shasta Dam construction projects. Chet Todd's family also moved to Redding that year. Todd and Dona Hanes met while students at Shasta High School in 1949 and were married in 1950. Two years later Todd joined his father-in-law as a floor sander.

They soon expanded the business to include installation of floors after purchasing a supply of oak from an Arkansas mill. Hanes and Todd formed a partnership in 1958 and added resilient flooring to the business, closely followed by carpet, ceilings, and countertops. Hanes sold his interest to Todd in 1962 and moved to Westwood, California, where he started a similar business, then subsequently opened a variety store. Fifteen years later he and Theo returned to Redding to enjoy retirement.

Todd incorporated the business, retaining the founder's name. His accomplishments were marred in 1965 by the untimely death of his wife, Dona.

Construction of a new Shasta College campus in 1967 produced the firm's first large contract, when Todd was the successful bidder on

Chet Todd, president of Hanes incorporated since 1963, has seen the firm grow to one of the largest building interior subcontracting companies in Northern California.

flooring and ceilings. Hanes incorporated gradually phased out of the residential field to concentrate on commercial projects. The firm has since performed a $250,000 subcontract for the remodeling at North Valley Plaza Mall in Chico, and regularly undertakes major jobs at military bases, schools, and hospitals in Northern California.

Todd married his present wife, Karen, in 1972, and Hanes incorpo-

rated has variously operated from each of the three buildings it owns on Commerce Street. Employment peaked in the 1970s, with a payroll of 40 people, but is presently about 15 employees, as the firm subcontracts more of its labor.

Among his many civic activities, Todd was president of the Shasta Builder's Exchange in 1984 and president of the Kiwanis Club of Redding in 1975. He has served on the board of directors of the YMCA and is a member of the building committee.

Hanes incorporated has undergone many changes on the way to becoming one of Northern California's largest building interior subcontracting companies. But two things that have not changed are Todd's commitment to family, and the family's commitment to Hanes incorporated. Brother-in-law Del Wellock, a 31-year employee, is job superintendent; sister Barbara Wellock is a bookkeeper; son Mark is an estimator; son Greg works for the firm out of Sacramento; and nephew Kim Wellock is an installer.

"I'm pleased that the company will continue as a family operation," Todd says. He plans to retire in 1990 and turn over direction of Hanes incorporated to Mark, Roy Hanes' grandson.

Hanes incorporated sold this 1948 Chevrolet panel truck for $50 to a local resident who neglected to paint out the sign. Chet Todd later repurchased the truck, along with two similar vehicles, for $1,000. It was restored and is retained as a historic vehicle.

NORTH VALLEY BANK

When North Valley Bank first opened its doors in 1973, there were no locally owned independent banks in the Redding area. At first North Valley operated from an 800-square-foot house on South Street between Market and Pine streets, but almost immediately began construction of its headquarters building adjacent to that tiny home/bank. With only 10 employees, the institution attracted nearly 5,000 accounts during its first three months of operations.

For the first six years North Valley Bank opened a new branch every year. Today, in addition to the original downtown bank, the institution has branches in Enterprise on Cypress Avenue and on Bechelli Lane, and in Central Valley, Westwood Village, Weaverville, Hayfork, and Anderson. Total accounts have grown to over 23,000, and assets exceed $75 million.

Herb Mueller, young, aggressive, and experienced in independent banking in the Bakersfield area, was chosen as the first president of North Valley Bank in 1972 during the chartering process and served until his retirement in October 1985. He was succeeded by Donald V. Carter, a graduate of Anderson High School, who began his banking career as a teller in a Redding national bank, later served in various capacities in Northern California and San Diego for that same bank, then spent nine years with an independent bank in Chico where he served as executive vice-president before accepting the North Valley Bank position.

Twelve of the bank's original 19 directors are still serving, with two lost through death and four through resignation. Current directors are Jack C. Alward, Rudy V. Balma, Earl B. Bibbens, Carter, Raymond V. Darby, Conrad J. Ferreira, Walter E. Glass, Alan T. Hill, William H. McDaniel, Bill G. Minton, Kelly V. Pierce, Richard K. Smart, and J.M. "Mike" Wells, Jr.

In 1982 all the directors of North Valley Bank to that time gathered for this group photo. They are (left to right, seated) Clair Hill, Herb Mueller, Earl Bibbens, Connie Ferreira, J.M. "Mike" Wells, Jr., and Rudy Balma. Middle row: Bill Minton, Alan Hill, John Perez (deceased), J.M. "Jim" Wells, Sr. (deceased), Bill McDaniel, Cigo Mazzini, and Dick Smart. In the rear row are Jaxon Baker, Ray Darby, Jack Alward, Ed Ochinero, Kelly Pierce, Ernie Glass, and Jim Campbell.

In 1981 North Valley Bank became a holding company, allowing it to diversify its operations. The parent firm is now North Valley Bancorp, with three subsidiaries—North Valley Bank, North Valley Trading Company, and North Valley Consulting Services.

"This is a local bank serving its local community," says Shirley Bickett, corporate affairs officer. "We want to take care of local people and help them buy their homes, buy their cars. We want to provide reasonable banking service in a professional manner."

Patrons

The following individuals, companies and organizations have made a valuable commitment to the quality of this publication. Windsor Publications and the Greater Redding Area Chamber of Commerce gratefully acknowledge their participation in *Redding & Shasta County: Gateway to the Cascades.*

Asher Veterinary Clinic
California Trailer & RV Supply
Laurence and Marie Carr
Cascade Union Elementary School District
Champion International Corp.
Citizens Utilities Company of California*
Country National Bank*
Cressey Beverage Distributing
C.M. Dicker, Inc.*
Economic Development Corp.
Joseph Russell Finazzo
Foothill Distributing Company, Inc.*
Franklin Engine & Part
Gandy, Scott, Tollefson & Company
Gerlinger's
Guiton's Pool Center
Hanes Incorporated*
Happy Fashions
Hempsted's Van & Storage
Jack F. Herrin
Hill & Cox, Inc.
Ironmongers Inc. Coast to Coast-Anderson
Johnson & Gamble
KMS Research Laboratories, Inc.*
KRCR 7R Television
Roy E. Ladd Construction Co.
Law Offices of Harrison Smith
John and Clara Lawson
Livingston Industries, Inc.*
McCollum Funding*
McDonald's Chapel/Redding Cemetery*
John Mackey Realty
Anton and Shirley Maier
Mrs. William Main
Marcoin Business Services
Mercy Medical Center*
Nichols, Melburg, and Rossetto,

A.I.A.*
North Valley Bank*
Northern California Plastic Surgery Medical Group, Inc.*
Northstar Aviation Center*
Nystrom & Company
Ott Water Engineers, Inc.
Paraclipse, Inc.*
Pepsi Cola Bottling Company*
Private Industry Council of Shasta County*
Record Searchlight
Redding Bank of Commerce
Redding Elementary School District*
Redding Family Medicine Associates
Redding Medical Center*
Redding Museum and Art Center
Redding Museum Store
Redding Paint Mart Inc.
Redding Parks and Recreation
Lee and Linda Salter
Joe Schneider, D.D.S.
Mr. and Mrs. Terrance Scott
Security Pacific National Bank
Deborah Shammo
Shamrock Equipment Co.
Sharrah Dunlap and Associates, Inc.*
Shascade Realty
Shasta County Library
Shasta County Private Industry Council
Shasta Siskiyou Transport*
Shasta Tile & Floor Covering
Sierra Pacific Industries
Simpson Paper Company*
Skyway Recreation Products*
State Compensation Insurance Fund
Sterling Guild-Shasta General Hospital
Sunset Plastics, Inc.*
Mr. and Mrs. Joseph A. Tellerico
Thrift Dry Cleaners
Robert S. Toenjes, D.D.S., Family Dentistry
Alice M. Trumbull Gift Shopping Service
Voorwood Company*
Wells Fargo Bank
Mr. and Mrs. Henry C. Woodrum

*Partners in Progress of *Redding & Shasta County: Gateway to the Cascades.* The histories of these companies and organizations appear in Chapter IX, beginning on page 135.

Bibliography

Allen, Marion V. *The Yana: An Indian Story.* Redding: C.P. Printing and Publishing, 1982.

Boggs, Mae Helene Bacon. *My Playhouse Was a Concord Coach.* Oakland: Howell-North Press, 1942.

Bowles, Samuel. *Our New West.* Hartford, Connecticut: Hartford Publishing Company, 1869.

Chase, Don M. *Pioneers.* Don M. Chase, 1945.

Colby, W. Howard. *A Century of Transportation in Shasta County.* Association for North County Resources and Research, 1982.

Covered Wagon. Various articles and 1980 Jubilee edition. Redding: Shasta Historical Society.

Eaton, Herbert. *The Overland Trail.* New York: Capricorn Books, G.P. Putnam and Sons, 1974.

Frank, B.F. and H.W. Chappell. *History and Business Directory for Shasta County.* Redding: Redding Independent Book and Job Printing House, 1881.

Freese, John R. *Redding: Origins and Development.* Master's thesis, California State University, Chico, 1983.

Gifford, Helen S. *Man of Destiny: Pierson Barton Reading.* Redding: Shasta Historical Society, 1985.

Giles, Rosena. *A History of Shasta County, California.* California Centennial Edition, 1949.

Gleeson, Charles J. *Outpost on Poverty Flat.* Redding: Redding Printing Company, 1978.

Knapp, Rufus R. *The Shutter Snaps.* San Antonio: Naylor Publishing Company, 1975.

Kutras, George C. *Shasta, California, A History.* Master's thesis, California State University, Chico, 1956.

McNamar, Myrtle. *Way Back When.* Hardback mimeograph, 1952. Revised 1963.

Meacham, A.B. *Wigman and Warpath.* Boston: John R. Dale & Company, 1875.

Peterson, Edward. *In the Shadow of a Mountain.* Hardback mimeograph. 1965.

————. *Redding: The First Hundred Years.* Redding: Redding Centennial Committee, North-Cal Printing and Litho, 1972.

Riddle, Jeff. *Indian History of the Modoc War.* Medford, Oregon: Pine Cone Publishers, reprint, 1973.

Ross, Albert F. *Record Searchlight.* Miscellaneous columns from the late 1960s.

Sanders, Bessie, et al. *A History of Shasta County, California.* Dallas: Taylor Publishing Company, 1985.

Satorius, Veronica. *Between the Lines.* The Catholic Church in Shasta County, California, 1853-1977. Portland, Oregon: Graphics Art Center, 1978.

Speer, J. Vern. *Involvement: Thumbnail Sketches.* Redding: North-Cal Printing and Litho, 1972.

Swartzlow, Ruby Johnson. *Lassen: His Life and Legacy.* Loomis Museum Association, 1964.

Wilsey, Roy E. *Hillbilly Boy: An Autobiography.* Redding: North-Cal Printing and Litho, 1971.

ARCHIVES
Courier Free-Press
Northern Argus
Red Bluff Sentinel
Redding Free Press
Redding Outlook
Redding Record
Redding Record Searchlight
Redding Searchlight
Sacramento Bee
Sacramento Union
Shasta Courier
Shasta Damboree
Yreka Daily Journal

Index

PARTNERS IN PROGRESS INDEX

Citizens Utilities Company of California, 168-169
Country National Bank, 150
Dicker, Inc., C.M., 142-143
Foothill Distributing Company, Inc., 167
Greater Redding Area Chamber of Commerce, 136
Hanes Incorporated, 177
KMS Research Laboratories, Inc., 170-171
Livingston Industries, Inc., 146-147
McCollum Funding, 159
McDonald's Chapel/Redding Cemetery, 137
Mercy Medical Center, 144-145
Nichols, Melburg, and Rossetto, A.I.A., 151
Northern California Plastic Surgery Medical Group, Inc., 174-175
Northstar Aviation Center, 156-157
North Valley Bank, 178
Paraclipse, Inc., 152-153
Pepsi Cola Bottling Company, 162-163
Private Industry Council of Shasta County, 138-139
Record Searchlight, 158
Redding Elementary School District, 172-173
Redding Medical Center, 140-141
Sharrah Dunlap and Associates, Inc., 166
Shasta Siskiyou Transport, 148-149
Simpson Paper Company, 160-161
Skyway Recreation Products, 176
Sunset Plastics, Inc., 164-165
Voorwood Company, 154-155

GENERAL INDEX
Italicized numbers indicate illustrations.

Afterthought Mine, 39
Ahjumawi Lava Springs State Park, 103
Aircraft, 108, 108, 109
Airports, 110
Air shows, 108, 109
Albro, George, 53, 62, 68
Alta Californian, 58
Alta House, 48
America balloon, 108, 109
Anderson, Roscoe, 68
Anderson-Cottonwood Irrigation District, 69
Anderson Water Company, 52
Anglo California Bank, 57
Atkinson Company, Guy F., 74
Automobile clubs, 5

Baird Caves, 95
Balaklala Copper Company, 39
Balaklala Mine, 37, 39
Balma, John, 64, 64, 65

Banking, 57
Bank of Northern California, 40, 57
Bartle Logging Company, J.J., 89
Battle Creek, 20
Battle of Bloody Island, 17
Battle of Castle Crags, 16, 17
Bear Flag Revolt, 22
Behrens, Charles, 62, 63
Bella Vista, 81
Benton Airpark, 109-110
Berry, Charles E., 111
Biegle, W.D., 115
Black Bart, 62, 63, 64
Black, Charles, James B., John, and Shirley Temple, 78
Blacks, 60, 61
Bloody Island, 13
Blumb, Henry, 47, 52
Bodenhamer, Paul C., 58
Bolton, Charles, 63, 63
Brickwood, Bill, 117
Briggsville, 27
Brokeoff Mountain, 128
Brown, Edmund G. "Pat," Sr., 92
Buckeye, 27
Buffalo Bill Cody's Wild West Show, 52
Bull, Baker and Company, 32
Bully Hill, 37
Bully Hill Mine, 36, 39
Buncombe's Mill, 20, 21
Bunker Hill Sawmill, 52, 82, 84
Bunyan Lumber Company, Paul, 90
Burney, 43
Burney Falls, 110
Bush, Chauncey Carroll "C.C.," 30, 31, 42, 42, 43, 46, 58, 60
Buzzard's Roost, 85, 87

California Street, 48
Camden, Charles, 36
Canby, Edward R.S., 21
Captain Jack, 20, 21, 43
Carnegie Library, 119
Carr, Francis Christopher, 69, 69
Carr, James K., 73
Carter, Harlan, Jesse, and Oliver, 130
Carter, W.O., 42, 61
Carter House Science Museum, 130, 131, 131
Castella, 44
Castle Crags, 6-7, 14, 125
Castle Crags battle, 19, 21
Castle Rock Mineral Springs Company, 50
Castle Rock Springs Hotel, 50
Catholics, 58
Centerville, 27
Central Pacific Railroad, 27, 41
Central Valley, 132

Central Valley Project, 70, 78
Champion International, 90, 91
Charles, George T., 117
Chase, A.R., 52, 82
Chiles-Walker party, 22
Chinese, 34, 41, 60
Christian Scientists, 60
Churches: African Methodist Episcopal Zion, 61; All Saints Episcopal, 61; Baptist, 59; Catholic, 60; Christian Methodist Episcopal, 61; Jesus Christ and the Latter-day Saints, 61; First Baptist, 60; First Presbyterian, 58, 60; Little Country, 61; Methodist, 60; Methodist Episcopal, 59; Pilgrim Congregational, 61; St. Joseph Catholic, 59, 61; Second Baptist, 61; Willing Workers Church of God, 61
Churntown, 27
Citizens Hook and Ladder Company No. 1, 46
City government, 121
City Livery Stable, 27
Clineschmidt, Henry "Hank," 104, 105, 106
Collyer, Gilbert, 129, 130
Communications, 111, 113
Congregationalists, 60
Copper City, 37
Copper mining, 36, 37, 39
Coram, 37, 39
Cottonwood Rodeo, 127
Covered Wagon, 17, 130
Covington, Virgil, 116
Cowden, Robert W., 117
Cowgill, J.S. "Sid," 115, 117
Crocker Bank, 57
Crystal Creek Conservation Camp, 65
Crystal Springs, 103

Daily Free Press, 113
Dams, building of, 67, 73, 75, 78. See also Shasta Dam
Deadwood Mine, 24
De La Mar, 37, 39
Deukmejian, George, 113
Diestelhorst, George, Isobel, and Mabel, 99
Diestelhorst Bridge, 15, 27, 28, 99
Diestelhorst Flat, 12
Dotta, James, 17
Dozier, Earnest "Doc," 58
Dunsmuir, 30, 105

Eagle Creek, 27
Earthquakes, 55, 89
Eaton's Drug Store, 113
Economic Development Corporation, 116, 117
Edkin, Robert W., 58
Empire Hotel, 5, 31

Energy, 78
Enterprise, 61
Ewing, Loren L., 56, *130*

Fahrni, Fred, 90
Fall River Mills, 43
Finn, Maurice "Moe," 117
Fires, 43, *45,* 46, 82
Fish and Game Commission, 27, 104, 105
Flooding, 67, 95
Fort Reading, 20, 21
Fort Ross, 16
Forty-Niners, 27
Frémont, John C., 17, *17,* 22
French Gulch, 27, 28, *28*
French Gulch Hotel, 29
French Gulch mine, 34
Frisbie, Edward, 42, *43,* 57, 60
Frisbie, Edward Charles, 57

Gard, Barbara, *118,* 121
Gerard, Lou, Sr., *133*
Gibbons and Reed Construction Company, 78
Gleeson, Charles J. "Chick," 58, 102
Glover's Garage, *54, 111*
Gold, discovery of, 17, 19, 25, 27, 30, 32, *35, 36, 39*
Golden Eagle Hotel, 56
Grange, The (store), 52
Great Fair of 1915, 56
Grotefend, A., 47, 52

Harrison, W.R., 27
Harrison Gulch, *26*
Hayes, Rutherford B., 52, 99
Hensley, Samuel, 22, 81
Hill, Clair A., 74, *74*
Hill, John B., 58, *59*
Hood, John Bell, *19,* 20
Hook and Ladder Company, 42
Hoover, Herbert, 99
Hoover Dam, 70
Horsetown, 27, 39
Hotel Redding, *44*
Hudson's Bay Company, 17
Hunt, Lucy, 118

Igo, 27, 58
Incorporation of Redding, 43, 47
Indians: Achomawi, 12, 13, *103;* Atsugewi, 12;
    Kientepoo, 21; Modoc, 12, 13, *20,* 21, 43;
    Pit, 13; Sastika, 16; Shasta, 12, 16; Wintu,
    11, 12, *12,* 13, *13,* 17, 21, 101; Yana, 12, 21
Ingot, 39
International Paper Company, 92
Iron Canyon Dam, 69
Iron Canyon project, 67

Iron Mountain, 36, 37, *37,* 39
Iron Mountain Mine, 56

Jehovah's Witnesses, 60
John P. Scripps Newspapers, 58
Josephine Lake, *121*
Journalism, 57, 58
Juvenile Hall, 65

Kaiser, Henry, 73
Kamloops Incorporated, 104, 105, 106
Kennedy, John F., 74, 78, *78, 79*
Kennett, 37, *38*
Keswick, William, 56
Keswick, 37
Keswick Dam, 77
Keswick Light and Power Company, 56
Kettlebelly, 27
Kilarc Power House, 67, *68*
Kimberly, John, 92
Kimberly-Clark Corporation, 92

Lake Britton, 104
Lake Redding Park, 130
Lake Shasta Caverns, *100*
LaMoine, *46,* 81
Lassen, Peter, 22, 31, 32
Lassen Park Ski Area, *112, 128*
Lassen Peak, *6-7,* 87, 95, *96,* 99
Lassen Volcanic National Park, 99, *113*
Lava Beds National Monument, 20
Law enforcement, 49, 61, 65, *65*
Lincecum, Scott, *64*
Litsch, Charles, *33*
Logging, *80,* 81, *82,* 84, *88,* 92. *See also*
    Timber industry
Loomis, B.F., *85,* 87, *96, 111*
Loomis Museum, B.F., 99
Louisiana-Pacific Corporation, 92
Lumber trade, 81, 89, *89,* 92
Lutherans, 60

McArthur, Ethel, Frank, and John, 110
McArthur-Burney Falls State Park, 110
McCloud, 17, 81, 92
McCloud Flat, *89*
McCloud-Pit project, 78
McColl, John, 69
McCormick-Saeltzer Company, 49, 50, *54,* 57,
    111
McLeod, Alexander, 16, 17
Mad River, 16
Mammoth Copper Company, 37, 55
Manton, 85
Mardon, Esther, 118
Market Street, *60, 73, 111*
Marler, Fred W., Jr., 115

Masonic Lodge, 30, *31,* 32
Massacre of Bloody Point, 21
Mercy Medical Center, *120,* 129
Methodists, 58
Middletown, 27
Miller, Cincinnatus "Joaquin," 16, *16,* 17, 33,
    58
Millville, 21, *45,* 85
Mining, 19, 27, 30, 33, 34, *34, 35, 47*
Montgomery Creek, 85
Mormons, 60
Mountain Copper Company, 36, 104
Mountain Lakes Industrial Park, 117
Mt. Lassen, *6-7, 10, 27*
Mt. Shasta, 16, 95, *124, 126*
Mt. Shasta Ski Bowl, 110
Mt. Shasta Ski Park, *113*
Muir, John, 95
Muletown, 27

National Medical Enterprises, Inc., 129
Nibarger Ranch, *51*
Noble, H.H., 56
Nobles' Trail, 32
Northern Argus, 39, 58
Northern California Power Association, 78
Northern California Power Company, 56, 67
North Star Mill, *45*
Novoply, 90, 91, *91*

Oak Bottom, 30
Ogden, Peter, 16
Ono, 27, *122*
Ono Justice Court, 33

Pacific Bell, 111
Pacific Constructors, Inc., 70
Pacific Gas and Electric Company, 56, 67, 70,
    78
Panama-Pacific Exposition, 56
Panic of 1893, 55
Peeples, W.A., 52, 82
Pennsylvania House Hotel, 52
Perez, John, 118
Petersen, Edward, 42
Pettijohn Mountain, 76
Piety Hill, 27, 58
Pit River, *107*
Plywood-Champion mill, 92
Pondosa, 81
Poole, L.D. "Lou," *45, 65*
Poverty Flat, 13, 16, 27, 49
Power companies, 67
Ptotem Creek Falls, *127*
Public Utilities Commission, 78

Radio Stations, 113

Railroads, 27, 30, 41, 42, *72*, 87
Rancho Buena Ventura, 17, 22, 23, 42
Reading, Pierson Barton, 13, 19, 20, 22, 23, *23*, 24, 28, 39, 42
Record Searchlight, 65, 76, 102, 110
Record Searchlight and Courier-Free Press, 58
Red Bluff, 16, 27
Redding, B.B., 27, *29*, 57, 58
Redding City Hall, 48
Redding Civic Auditorium and Civic Center, *123*
Redding Foundry and Machine Works, 52
Redding Hotel, 42
Redding Medical Center, 56, *120*, 129
Redding Municipal Airport, 110
Redding Museum & Art Center, *130*, 130
Redding Planing Mill, 52, 82
Redding Record, 58
Redding Reduction Works, 52
Redding Savings Bank, 57
Red River Lumber Company, 89
Reginato, John, 106
Reid Mine, 39
Reid's Ferry, 27, *28*
Resort hotels, 99
Richardson, James A., 101
Richardson, James L., *62*, 63
Rodeo Week Parade, *123*
Roop, Isaac, 30
Roop's War, 30
Roosevelt, Theodore, 95, 110
Roseburg Lumber Company, 92
Russ, Albert F., 53, 56
Round Mountain, 81, 85, 87
Royal T. Sprague Mine, *34*
Ruggles, Charlie, and John, 62

Sacramento River, *15*, *126;* canyon, 36
St. Caroline Hospital, 121
St. Charles Hotel, 32
Salmon Wars, 19
Sanders, Bessie, 118, *118*
Sawmills, 81, 82, *83*, 84, 85
Schools: Little Pine Street, 50, *50;* Nova High, *130;* Shasta College, 130, 131; Shasta Community College, *129;* Shasta High, 50, 55, *56*, 129, 130, 131
Scott, John V., 47, 52
Seventh-day Adventists, 60
Shasta Cascade Wonderland Association, 106
Shasta County Courthouse, 52, *53*, 55, *63*, 68
Shasta County Promotion and Development Association, 69
Shasta County Recorder's Office, *47*
Shasta County Superior Court, 91
Shasta Courier, 30, 42, 47, 58, 61

Shasta Dam, 39, 58, *66*, 68, 69, 70, *71*, *72*, 73, 74, 84, 95, 102, 106, *126*
Shasta Dam Area Chamber of Commerce, 102
Shasta Dam Boulevard, *132*
Shasta Dial, 58
Shasta General Hospital, 129
Shasta Historical Monument, 58
Shasta Historical Society, 17
Shasta Lake, *94*, 95, 102, *102*, 104, *126*
Shasta-Trinity Divide, *26*
Shasta Union High School District, 130
Sheridan, George, and family, *84*
Sheridan, L.O., *84*
Sheridan, Philip Henry, *18*, 19, 20
Shingletown, 85
Sholes, Earl, *64*
Shurtleff, Benjamin, 22, 30
Silica mining, 39
Silver mining, 39
Simon and Brothers, I., 52
Simpson Lee Paper Company, 92
Skiing, 110, 111, *112*, *113*, *128*
Smith, Jedediah, 16
Smith, Warren, 90
Smith Lumber Company, Ralph L., 90, *90*, 92
Southern Pacific Railroad, *72*
Southern's (resort hotel), 99
Stamp mills, 25
Star-Free Press, 58
State Board of Fish Commissioners, 27
State Water Plan, 70
State Water Project, 74
Steelhead Unlimited, 104, 106
Stevenson, B.E., 46, 62
Stillwater Plains, 110
Storm, Phil W., 117
Strikes, 92
Student Training Orientation Program (Stop), 65
Sugarloaf, 104
Sulfur mining, 36
Sunset Telephone Company, 111
Sutter, John A., *18*, 23
Sutter's Fort, 22
Sutter's Mill, 19

Telephone service, 111, 113
Television, 113
Temple Hotel, 50, 104, *105*
Temple Street, *60*
Terry Lumber Company, *80*, 85, *86*, 87
Texas Springs, 27, 58
Thatcher, Art, and family, *85*
Thatcher, Ezekial and Tom, 85
Thatcher Lumber Company, 85
Timber industry, *83*, *93*, 122. See also

Logging
Trappers, 17
Trinity Alps, 95
Trinity Centre Hotel, *26*
Trinity Lake, *98-99*, 102
Trinity River Project, 74, *75*, 76, 77, *77*, 78, 95
Trojan Horse Rock, *14*

Unitarians, 60
U.S. Bureau of Indian Affairs, 20
U.S. Highway 99, 107
U.S. Plywood Corporation, 90

Vanderpool, George, 64
Viola, 85, 87

Warren's Diamond Bar Saloon, Slim, 37, *37*, 38
Washington Mine, 34
Weaverville, 43
Weed, 81, 92
Wells Fargo Bank, 57
Whiskey Creek, 29, 30
Whiskeytown, 29, *29*, 77
Whiskeytown Dam, 77, 78, *78*, *79*
Whiskeytown Lake, 29, *76*, 77, 102, *114*, *124*
Whiskeytown Regatta, 78
Whitmore, *84*
Whitmore Hotel, 84
Work, John, 16
World War I, 56
World War II, 113
Wright's Garage, 104
Wyatt, Thomas "Doc," 56, 129

Yreka, 30

Zinc, 36

The Gold That Grew By Shasta Town

By Joaquin Miller

From Shasta town to Redding town
the ground is torn by miners, dead:
the Manzanita, rank and red
drops dusty berries up and down
their grass-blown trails, their silent mines
are wrapped in Chaparral and vines;
yet one gray miner still sits down
'twixt Redding and sweet Shasta town.

The quail pipes pleasantly. The hare
leaps careless o'er the golden oat
that grows beneath the water moat;
the lizard grows below in sunlight there.
The brown hawk swims the perfumed air
unfrightened through the livelong day;
and now and then a curious bear
comes shuffling down the ditch by night.

And leaves some wide, long trace on clay
so human-like, so stealthy light,
where one lone cabin still stoops down
'twixt Redding and sweet Shasta town.

That great graveyard of hopes! Of men
who sought for hidden veins of gold:
of young men dead, sudenly grown old—
of old men dead, despairing when
the gold was just within their hold!
that storied land, whereon the light
of other days gleams faintly still;
some like the halo of a hill
that lifts above the fading night.
That warm, red, rich and human land,
that flesh-red soil, that warm red sand,
where one gray miner still sits down
'twixt Redding and sweet Shasta town.